The Craft of Editing

Springer
New York
Berlin
Heidelberg
Barcelona
Hong Kong
London
Milan
Paris
Singapore
Tokyo

The Craft of Editing

A Guide for Managers, Scientists, and Engineers

Michael Alley

Springer

Michael Alley
College of Engineering
Virginia Tech
Blacksburg, VA 24061-0238
USA
http://www.me.vt.edu/writing/

Cover illustrations: The space shuttle *Discovery* on July 13, 1995. On this flight, the main engine was supplied by high-pressure, liquid-oxygen turbopumps developed by Pratt & Whitney. Pictured in the upper right frame is the hydrogen-fuel turbopump (still to be flown), pictured in the lower right frame is the oxidizer turbopump, and pictured in the middle right frame is the shuttle's thrust chamber. Photos courtesy of Pratt & Whitney, Liquid Space Propulsion, a United Technologies company. In this book, discussions about editing illustrations occur on pages 59 and 109.

Library of Congress Cataloging-in-Publication Data
Alley, Michael.
    The Craft of editing : a guide for managers, scientists, and engineers / Michael Alley.
      p.   cm.
    Includes bibliographical references.
    ISBN 0-387-98964-1 (soft cover : alk. paper)
    1. Technical editing.   I. Title
  T11.4.A43   2000
  808´.0666—dc21   99-056072

Printed on acid-free paper.

Production managed by Lesley Poliner; manufacturing supervised by Joe Quatela.
Photocomposed copy produced using files prepared by the author.
Printed and bound by R.R. Donnelley and Sons, Harrisonburg, VA.
Printed in the United States of America.

9 8 7 6 5 4 3 2 1

ISBN 0-387-98964-1 Springer-Verlag New York Berlin Heidelberg   SPIN 10750681

For my brother and sister

Preface

You are a hired gun of sorts: a manager, scientist, or engineer called upon to edit a document. Perhaps you are overseeing a long report or thesis, reviewing a journal article, or providing comments on a proposal. For the document before you, what changes do you suggest? How do you clearly and efficiently communicate those changes to the author? How do you convince the author and the other editors that those changes are needed? The answers to these questions define how you edit someone's writing.

In business, engineering, and science, the process of editing causes much strife. In fact, my experience in teaching professional writing over the past fifteen years has been that editing is the number one complaint that professionals have about the process of documenting their work. Many professionals complain that this editing seems to arise more from whim than from logic — that what flies in one document is often shot down in another. Others complain that editors change too much, essentially inserting their own individual styles. Still others complain that the sign-off process is so inefficient and taxing that they sometimes do not document work they know should be documented. While in many cases these complaints are unfounded, in many others they are legitimate. This book addresses those complaints that are legitimate by showing managers, scientists, and engineers how to make their editing both more effective and more efficient.

So what exactly does this book provide? First, when you sit down to edit someone's writing, your goal is to work with that author to strengthen the writing as much as possible. To be an effective and efficient editor, you have to understand what within the document you should change and what you should not. This book provides you with that understanding.

Once you understand what to change in the writing, you have to assess the level to which you should change it. To help you determine this level, this book analyzes the three types of editorial changes made on documents: changes in content, changes in style, and changes in form. In doing so, the book helps you gauge how far in each category to go. Moreover, to show you how to communicate your changes to authors, this book works through four editing situations in which managers, scientists, and engineers often find themselves: reviewing, copyediting on paper, copyediting on a computer, and proofreading.

Yet another topic that the book discusses is the process of editing from the institution's perspective. In analyzing this topic, this book recommends strategies for making the sign-off process more efficient. In addition to discussing the physical aspects of editing, the book discusses a key psychological aspect of editing: the friction that often arises between the editor and the author. Finally, the book contains a guide that tackles one hundred problems of style that managers, scientists, and engineers often confront as editors. In presenting this guide, I have assessed not only how much controversy surrounds each problem, but also the relative importance of each problem in the larger context of informing and persuading an audience.

Why choose this book on editing? One reason is that the advice in this book is based on actual editing experiences from business, engineering, and science. Because the advice arises from actual documents, you will find that it is practical, straightforward, and tested. Another reason to choose this book is that it does not try to cover the gamut of editing as experienced by professional editors. Rather, the book focuses on the kind of editing that you as a manager, scientist, or engineer experience. That focus is you, your pencil (or computer), and someone else's writing.

I wish that I could tell you that this book will make your editing easy. No book could honestly make such a claim. Your editing will be a struggle for precision—fraught with language conundrums and harrowed by deadlines. Nonetheless, a well-edited document is a worthy goal. Such a document benefits your institution, your author, and you.

In writing this book, I owe much to the following individuals at Springer-Verlag: Dr. Thomas von Foerster, my editor; David Kramer, my copy editor; and Lesley Poliner, my production editor. In addition, I received valuable input from several colleagues: Harry Robertshaw, from Virginia Tech; Rea Dahm, from RMT; Harold Bradley, from Enron; and Brad Hughes and Frank Siciliano, from the University of Wisconsin. Also advising me were three members of my family: my wife, who is on the mechanical engineering faculty at Virginia Tech; my mother, a retired chemistry professor; and my father, who for five years served as plant manager of the Mason-Hanger Pantex Plant. Finally, I am indebted to those individuals who participated in my writing courses over the past fifteen years. Their comments, criticisms, and suggestions have served to edit my work.

Michael Alley
Blacksburg, Virginia
November 1999

Contents

Chapter 1

Editing:
Where Do You Begin?

There is no greater desire in the world than to change someone else's writing.

Robert Louis Stevenson

The pilot has removed the *fasten seat belt* sign, the man in the aisle seat beside you has stopped his nervous chatter, and you are ready to begin editing Calloway's report. Before the flight attendants even begin the beverage service, the report has you rattled. The problems you see are certainly not insurmountable, but they are distracting. First is the text typeface, a large sans serif font that would be appropriate perhaps for an elementary school reader, but not for a technical report, especially not for one with national distribution. Another distraction is Calloway's penchant for pretentious words: *prioritization, facilitation,* and *manufacturability*. These words make the document read like something written by a bureaucrat, not by an engineer. Still another distraction is Calloway's confusion between *affect* and *effect*. How could an engineer who reads even the minimum amount of literature in his or her field make that mistake?

You try to focus on larger issues of content such as whether Calloway is divulging proprietary information, but the word choices and *Romper Room* typeface distract you. Like a poison ivy itch, they prick and needle you from Atlanta to the Great Smoky Mountains. By the time the beverage cart arrives, you are bearing down so hard on your pencil that your editing marks leave permanent indentations on the pages beneath. More than once, you have spoken to Calloway about these matters, but he does not share your sensitivity.

In your briefcase are three other documents that you intend to edit on this trip. You consider switching to one of them, but do not. Calloway's has the highest priority, if for no other reason than it is the one furthest behind schedule. The flight attendant asks you what you would like to drink, and you select something cold with bubbles.

Knowing Your Goals

When you sit down to edit someone's document, the goal is straightforward: to improve the document as much as can be expected, given the constraints, such as deadlines, under which the document exists. Although the goal is clear, obtaining the goal poses a challenge because documents can be viewed from such different perspectives.

One perspective is content, or what message the author intends. A second perspective is style, or how well the message is said. Yet a third perspective is form, which encompasses the format,* grammar, punctuation, spell-

---

*Editing terms are defined in the Glossary.

ing, and usage of the message. As shown in Table 1-1, several issues are associated with each of these perspectives. Note that for each issue we could develop an even more detailed level of subissues. In fact, many professional editors write out that next level. That next level is not universal, though. Rather, it depends on several factors, including the audience, the purpose, and the occasion. Given that, we will stop at this level for now.

Not all of these three perspectives (content, style, and form) hold the same importance. While this book spends much of its ink on style and form, content is essential for successful communication. If the message is incorrect, then the document fails, no matter how well the message is communicated or what form it is in. Consider the case

Table 1-1. Perspectives of Editing.

Perspectives	Key issues
Editing for content	Information correct? Information complete? Information appropriate for the audience? Information appropriate for the purpose? Information acceptable for distribution?
Editing for style	Organization sound? Transitions smooth? Emphasis proper? Language clear? Illustrations clear?
Editing for form	Format consistent? Grammar correct? Punctuation correct? Usage proper? Spelling correct?

of an internal memorandum issued by Dow Corning in 1975. That year, Dow Corning had created a task force to develop a new gel for the silicone breast implants it manufactured. On the task force, concern arose over whether this new gel leaked more than the older gel did. Echoing this concern were reports from salespeople who claimed that the new implants had oily coatings on the envelopes. One task-force member, on his own, responded to the salespeople with a memo stating that these oily coatings arose not from leakage, but from handling, and that the salespeople should continually change the demonstration samples to hide the oily feel. Because the memo ignored the genuine concern that the task force had about the leakage, the memo was "duplicitous" [Angell, 1996]. In later tort suits against Dow Corning, including a San Francisco suit in which the plaintiff won more than $7 million, this memo severely damaged Dow Corning's defense. The duplicity in this memo was clearly an aspect of content that Dow Corning regretted not having had the chance to edit.

Editing for content requires that you consider the accuracy and completeness of the information. After all, if the results are suspect or if conclusions are reached without sufficient data, then embarrassment, or worse, could ensue. In addition to checking for accuracy and completeness, editing for content includes other aspects that depend on the situation. One aspect is whether the information is appropriate for the audience. In other words, is the information too technical, or not technical enough? Interwoven with the question of audience is the question of purpose: Is the information appropriate for the document's purpose? Not all professional writing has the sole purpose of informing. Many professional documents are written to convince. For that reason, an editor should assess whether the writing achieves that purpose, and if not, then how it might best do so. Still another aspect of content that depends on the situation is whether the information is appropriate for distribution. For instance, does the document contain proprietary information? Or does the document state something that may be accurate, but is unacceptable to release (information classified as top secret, for example).

Besides the perspective of content, a second perspective for editors is style. While editing for content focuses on what is communicated, editing for style focuses on how well that message is presented. Another way to view this difference is that content is the freight train with the goods, and style is the track on which the train delivers the goods to the audience. Style is as necessary as content for successful communication. After all, what good is an idea if the person who conceives the idea does not communicate it effectively to others?

In assessing style, many questions arise. Are the details organized logically? Are transitions made between the details? Are key details emphasized? Is the language clear? Are the illustrations clear? Because so many questions are associated with the perspective of style, you cannot address them all. Rather, you should develop a hierarchy for the questions. A document with logical organization, smooth transitions, proper emphasis, and clear language and illustrations will succeed in informing the audience. If the language is also concise and fluid, the document will inform more efficiently, but success depends on the characteristics mentioned first.

While the first two perspectives — content and style — ensure that the appropriate message reaches the audience, the third perspective, form, affects the efficiency and authority of that delivery. Form includes the format, grammar, punctuation, usage, and spelling. If the form is inappropriate, the audience becomes distracted and unnecessarily bogged down. How you address this third perspective of form depends on the audience and the occasion. People have different sensitivities for correctness. For instance, American English allows for both *ensure* and *insure* to have the meaning "to make certain." British English, on the other hand, allows only *ensure* to have this meaning. As an editor, assessing the correctness of the writing's form means deciding whether using *insure* to mean "to make certain" distracts the intended audience. If so, then the usage does not serve the document, because it has moved the reader's attention away from the content to the writing itself. In such cases, you as an editor should select *ensure*, which has the intended meaning in both American and British English.

Note that you can become too sensitive to rules of form. Such a hypersensitivity to the rules can keep you from noticing other, more egregious, errors. Although many aspects of form such as splitting infinitives, using "impact" as a verb, and choosing a typeface such as Geneva for the text of a formal report might grate on readers, focusing too much of your editing attention on such aspects can cause you to miss factual errors and ambiguities — two aspects that are much more likely to upset and confuse the audience.

Knowing Your Constraints

In revising your own work, if you see a change that will improve the work, you usually just make it. In editing, though, if you see a change that will improve the work, you assess the effect of that change on the author, the other editors who will follow you, and the remainder of the writing. That is not to say that you lower your standards and allow clear-cut mistakes to pass through. What it means is that you weigh the variables shown in Figure 1-1 before advocating the change.

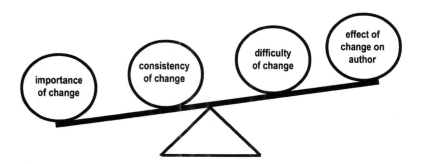

Figure 1-1. Variables balanced by an editor of a professional document.

One variable is the importance of the change. If the change is truly important with regard to content, style, or form, then you advocate it. As far as assessing whether a content change is important, you in your role as manager, scientist, or engineer draw upon your experience and education. As far as assessing whether changes in style or form are important, you draw upon your writing experience and education. For many managers, scientists, and engineers that second pool of knowledge from which to draw is not as deep as the first. This book, particularly Chapter 3 and the Appendix, attempts to deepen this second pool of knowledge.

Another variable to weigh in deciding whether to advocate an editorial change is whether the change is consistent with other aspects of content, style, and form in the document. For a content change such as expressing a measurement with more accuracy, a consistency question arises over whether other measurements in the document have been expressed to that number of significant digits. If not, then the accuracy of that measurement will be suspect. For a stylistic change such as using the first person ("I" or "we") in a particular sentence, a consistency question arises over whether first person has been used in similar situations throughout the document. If not, the use in that one situation might seem out of place. For a form change such as dropping the series comma from a list of three or more items, a consistency question arises over whether the series comma has been used in all lists throughout the document. If so, dropping it from the one list might unsettle the reader who has come to expect it.

A third variable is the difficulty of the change. For instance, when a hard deadline draws near, you have to challenge edits that will entail the author making major changes. Otherwise, you could end up with a document at the piecemeal stage when the document should be at the polishing stage. Such was the case several years ago at Garrett Turbine. On a multimillion dollar proposal to the Department of Energy, Garrett Turbine was clearly the front-runner for the contract, but Garrett attempted some major editing just a few days before the deadline. To allow time for this major editing, Garrett banked on an employee flying to Washington, D.C., on the due date and hand-delivering the proposal. Unfortunately, a thunderstorm in St. Louis delayed the employee on the final leg of the journey. What resulted was that the employee was late arriving at the Department of Energy and that the proposal was not accepted for consideration. In the end, Rolls-Royce garnered the contract.

A fourth variable in editing a professional document is the effect of the change on the author. For instance, a change that might seem small to you, who have just read the document for the first time, might appear huge to the author, who has struggled with the document for the past two months. In other words, your energy for the document might be much higher than that of the author, who will have to make the changes. How do you motivate the author to make the changes necessary? Chapter 5 delves into this question and other similar questions regarding the relationship between editor and author.

As has been discussed in this chapter, editors should consider several variables before expending pencil lead (traditionally, blue) on an edit. Also, editors should remember that the principal goal of editing is not to identify every error, but to convince the author and other editors to produce the best possible document, given the existing constraints. For the successful editor, realizing the constraints of the edit becomes second nature, a subconscious process that occurs before the blue pencil is even sharpened.

Chapter 2

When the Pencils Are Blue

Editing isn't a cosmetic process. It's a thinking process.
Richard Rhodes

As stated in the previous chapter, editors make three distinctive types of edits: content edits, stylistic edits, and form edits. Content edits address what documents say. These edits often affect large-scale decisions about documents, such as whether to accept them for publication, or whether the authors are headed in the appropriate directions. Stylistic edits address how the messages are delivered in documents. These edits focus on the structure, language, and illustration of documents. Finally, form edits address the appearances of documents. In other words, do the documents follow the accepted rules of grammar, punctuation, usage, spelling, and format?

As a manager, scientist, or engineer, you usually have to consider more than one of these perspectives while editing a document. Although you usually edit from more than one perspective, it is instructive to isolate the editing of each perspective. The reason is that by doing so you are in a much better position to organize your edits. Often when you edit a document, you end up with several concerns that you would like the author to address. By knowing how to catalogue these concerns, you can present them in a more logical fashion to the author. Not only will your author find it easier to follow your edits, but your author will be more likely to believe that your edits have arisen from logic, rather than whim.

Editing for Content

Managers, scientists, and engineers are often called upon to edit for content. One example is an in-house review of a proposal. Another example is the review of a paper for journal publication. In a content edit you focus on the message itself:

Is the information correct?
Is the information complete?
Is the information appropriate for the audience?
Is the information appropriate for the purpose?
Is the information acceptable for distribution?

The institution or journal for which you are editing may phrase these questions differently, but the focus of any content edit will be on the message itself.

How to Structure a Content Edit. Content edits are often written as stand-alone critiques rather than comments scattered through a document. For that reason, how you structure a content edit is important. In structuring a stand-alone content edit, you want to achieve two main goals: (1) make sure that the author and other editors clearly know your overall stand on the document; and (2) make sure that the author and other editors understand the relative importance of your criticisms. One of the best ways to achieve the first goal is to state your overall stand early in the content edit. This statement might seem unnecessary, but many content edits, especially reviews of journal papers, suffer from being cryptic, focusing on tangential points in the paper and skirting the question of whether the paper should be published. By stating your overall stand early in your content edit, you avoid making your content edit a mystery in which you keep the author and other editors in suspense (and confusion) about your assessment until the last sentence.

The second goal for the structure of a content edit is that you show the relative importance of your criticisms. To show this relative importance, you should avoid long lists of criticisms (more than five items), because items in long lists are often missed. While such a list might be fine for a form edit in which the author corrects each mistake one at a time at the sentence level, having a long list in a content edit often creates confusion, because content critiques usually address issues found throughout the document. Moreover, the relative importance of items in a long list is difficult to distinguish. The longer the list is, the more that it appears as if each item in the list holds equal rank.

What happens, though, if you have eight criticisms? In such a situation, you should group your criticisms in some way. For instance, four of your criticisms might address the experimental technique, two of your criticisms might address the error analysis, and two of your criticisms might address the presentation of the data. You can use paragraphs or sections to separate these groups. If one group is more important than the other, place it first. Likewise, if one criticism within a group is more important than others, place it first within that group. What happens if no logical groupings of your criticisms exist? In such a case, use headings such as "Major Criticisms" and "Minor Criticisms" so that you do not bury your major criticisms in a long list of minor points.

How to Phrase a Content Edit. In writing or delivering a content edit, the editor should work to control tone, which in an edit is the attitude that you, the editor, show toward the document and the author. Often in a content edit, you suggest changes that require much work from the author: (1) adding major portions, (2) cutting major portions, (3) rearranging major portions, and (4) reconsidering the audience. Because all of these requests require significant work for the author, you should be sensitive to the effect that these requests will have on the author. For that reason, give the author credit where credit is due. In other words, in your initial overall assessment, do not mention only what is weak, but also what is strong. You might consider this information unnecessary, but for many people, comments on their writing translate to personal assessments.

This advice of giving credit where credit is due does not mean that you lavish false praise upon someone or that for every sentence of criticism there is a corresponding sentence of praise — the lion's share of your edit will focus on the weaknesses. Rather, this advice means that in the beginning of your assessment you acknowledge what the author has done well. Recognizing the worth of the author's work increases your credibility with the author. If your edit were to contain only criticisms, the author might assume that you had missed the main points or, worse yet, that you had political motives against the document. Granted, in situations where the author's initial assumptions are false, finding something positive to say about the work, other than acknowledging the challenge of the work, may prove difficult. Still, by acknowledging that the work was challenging, you have built an important bridge to the author.

Controlling tone is not confined to the initial assessment. Throughout the edit, you have to be careful about your attitude toward the document and toward the author. Although you sometimes have to be stern to convey the importance of a criticism, you should never be condescending or belittling. For a professional, there is no place for those attitudes. In a recent review of a paper submitted to an engineering conference, the reviewer began with the following sentence: "This paper appears to have been written by a Russian clown." This sentence does not serve the review in any fashion. It serves only to alienate the author (and to denigrate Russian circus performers, who are some of the best in the world). Moreover, such a sentence suggests that the reviewer has not written the review to assess the paper, but to show his or her supposed superiority over the writer.

So how do you phrase suggested changes? The most straightforward way is to state the changes as additions or deletions that the authors should make:

> Figures 3, 5, 8, and 9 should have an expanded x-axis. It is not possible for the reader to identify trends in the data using the current scaling.

Another way that is not quite so forward is to word the changes as questions that the authors should address:

> Does the overall uncertainty estimate of ±0.3°C at 30°C, as listed on page 17, represent the bias error only, the precision error only, or the combination of bias and precision errors?

No matter which way you word the suggestion, the reason for the suggestion should be clear. Even in a situation in which you have uncontested authority to make changes, you should justify your changes so that the author sees that the changes are based on logic, not whim, and so that the author can learn from the changes. After all, the author may very well work on other documents that you will have to edit.

Besides controlling tone, you should anchor general criticisms with convincing examples. For instance, do not just say that the authors should provide more interpretation of the results. Anchor this generality with specifics:

> The authors have not interpreted the results enough. For instance, in Figure 8, which presents plots of the local Sherwood number ratios, no symmetry exists either at the entrance or in the fully

developed region. Neither these contour plots nor the accompanying discussions in the text explain this lack of symmetry.

What is the greatest editing challenge in a content edit? Probably the most difficult type of content editing is recognizing when something is missing from the document. This type of editing calls upon you to identify what is not on the page, rather than to correct what is. Such an edit requires that you not only understand the work, but also imagine what it should be.

Editing for Style

Editing for style in professional writing is challenging because style refers to so many different aspects of writing — from the arrangement of sections in the document to the arrangement of words within a sentence. Even more challenging, many stylistic aspects depend on the document's audience and purpose. Before we discuss how to edit for style, we should establish as clearly as possible what style is. One breakdown for style is shown in Figure 2-1. Here, style comprises three categories: structure, language, and illustration.

Structure is the strategy of the writing. In professional writing, structure encompasses not only the organization of details, but also the emphasis of details, the depth of details, and the transitions between details on the section and subsection levels. The second category, language, is the way that words are used on the sentence and paragraph levels. Successful language has several traits — it is

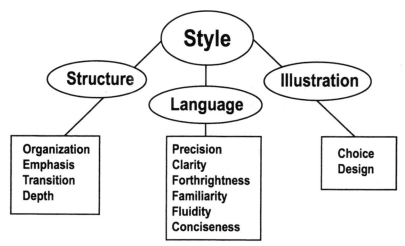

Figure 2-1. Aspects of style in professional writing.

precise, clear, forthright, familiar, fluid, and concise. Illustration, the third category, is the meshing of images and tables with the document's text. What makes for successful illustration? First, the type of illustration (photograph, drawing, diagram, graph, or table) should be appropriate for the situation, and second, the design of that illustration should be precise, clear, familiar, and fluid.

As mentioned, much about style depends on the document. With instructions, for example, paragraphs tend to be shorter because the principal focus is simply on how the process occurs. In reports and journal papers, paragraphs are longer because the principal questions include *why* as well as *how*. Also, with instructions, you are likely to see numbered lists that are arranged vertically and with white space. Such lists serve a set of instructions because the audience often reads a step and then turns away and performs the step. The numbering and the white space help the reader find his or her place in the instructions. In reports and articles, though, the audience reads in a more continuous fashion and for longer stretches. For that reason, vertical lists are not as desirable, since they break up the reading.

A common source of confusion in editing documents in business, engineering, and science occurs when someone uses writing principles that are appropriate in literary writing but not professional writing. While some traits of strong professional writing overlap with those of strong literary writing, many differences exist. Figure 2-2 shows a general hierarchy for the goals of language in professional writing. In this hierarchy, precision ranks as the most important goal. The reasoning is that in professional writing, communicating what actually occurs is crucial to understanding the content. In literary writing, though, precision does not rank as highly. For instance, a poet might choose the word "weight" as opposed to "mass" because of its sound. Likewise, while the sound of the

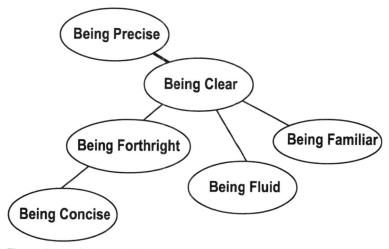

Figure 2-2. A hierarchy of language goals in professional writing.

writing is usually not an issue in professional writing, it is important for the literary writer. The fiction writer Evan Connell, for instance, claims that he has spent thirty minutes deciding whether to place an adjective before or after the noun that it modifies.

How to Structure a Stylistic Edit. Structuring a stylistic edit usually goes one of two ways. For situations in which your concerns are strictly on the sentence level, you might very well note your concerns on the document as they arise (for examples, see the sections on copyediting in Chapter 4). However, if the concerns are larger and pertain to entire sections, then you would probably want to rank those concerns on a separate sheet of paper in the way that you ranked concerns about content in the previous section. Likewise, you would want to keep your list relatively short (no more than five concerns), so that your most important concerns stand out. Should you have seven large stylistic concerns, you might group those concerns into categories — one grouping, for instance, might be organization of details, precision of language, clarity of language, and design of illustrations.

Note that the frequency of a stylistic flaw may cause you to mention it first, even though the flaw itself is not necessarily that high in importance. For instance, you might emphasize the need for more sentence variety, an aspect of secondary importance, if the document severely lacks that aspect. In a long paper in which the writer begins too many sentences the same way, the rhythm can become so monotonous that the reading slows to a crawl:

> Mount St. Helens erupted on May 18, 1980. A cloud of hot rock and gas surged northward from its collapsing slope. The cloud devastated more than 500 square kilometers of forests and lakes. The effects of Mount St. Helens were well documented with geophysical instruments. The origin of the eruption is not well understood. Volcanic explosions are driven by a rapid expansion of steam. Some scientists believe the steam comes from groundwater heated by the magma. Other scientists believe the steam comes from water originally dissolved by the magma. We have to understand the source of steam in volcanic eruptions. We have to determine how much water the magma contains.

In such a situation, advocating more variety in the way that sentences begin could well be the suggestion you emphasize most.

How Far to Take a Stylistic Edit. As mentioned, stylistic edits encompass many aspects of the writing. A difficulty for an editor is deciding how far to take a stylistic edit. In other words, at what point do you decide no more marks? The answer is not easy. Much depends on the document's importance and the time you have for the edit.

One thing that helps me decide how far to take a stylistic edit of a report is the checklist shown in Figure 2-3. This checklist, which has evolved from editing scores of reports, contains stylistic points that I find myself referring to time and again. In this checklist, the stylistic points are keyed to page numbers in my writing textbook [1996], to which I refer authors for additional information.

How do I use the checklist? Before editing, I review

Checklist for Stylistic Errors in Reports

Structure

Title:
    does not orient (17)
    is too long (18)
Introduction:
    does not define scope (27)
    does not show importance (28)
    does not give background (30)
    does not map (31)
Conclusion:
    does not analyze (41)
    does not provide closure (41)
Transitions into sections:
    first sentences abrupt (55)
    reader not oriented (54)

Summary:
    does not map, if descriptive (22)
    does not inform, if informative (23)
Middle:
    strategies illogical (33)
    headings not descriptive (38)
    headings not parallel (39)
    depth inappropriate (59)
Appendices:
    are not introduced in text (49)
    do not stand alone (47)
Emphasis of results:
    repetition not used well (64)
    placement not used well (66)

Language

Imprecision, word choice (73)
Needless complexity:
    in word choice (84)
    in noun phrases (85)
    in sentence structures (86)
Too many abstract nouns (102)
Tone not controlled (97)
Terms undefined (112)
Needless words (119)

Imprecision, level of detail (78)
Ambiguities:
    from word order (92)
    from unclear pronouns (93)
    from punctuation error (94)
Too many passive verbs (104)
Discontinuity:
    from stagnant rhythms (129)
    from poor transitions (137)

Illustration

Illustration is not introduced (162)
Illustration is not discussed (164)
Illustration does not mesh (164)
Caption is not specific (163)

Illustration is misplaced (167)
Illustration raises question (161)
Label is missing or incorrect (162)
Caption has incorrect form (163)

Figure 2-3. A checklist for common stylistic errors in reports. The numbers in parentheses refer to pages in *The Craft of Scientific Writing* [Alley, 1996].

the checklist so that those stylistic points are fresh in my mind. After editing the document, I look over the checklist again to make sure that I have not missed anything. This checklist is for reports. With special documents such as proposals, I modify the checklist to account for stylistic differences. For instance, with proposals, I often include phrases that refer to the strengths of the arguments.

In your own editing, you should develop your own list because the process of doing so forces you to define those stylistic aspects that you consider most important. The depth to which you want to go (or have time to go) will be reflected by the number of items you include.

Besides deciding how far to take an edit, another difficulty in editing for style is differentiating between suggestions considered universal and suggestions that are matters of individual taste. Here, the question comes down to whether the edit improves the communication to the audience or follows the individual preference of the editor. For instance, if we encountered the following sentence, most of us would identify the same problem:

> Enormous, high tech, modern mining companies are both continuing operations at old mines, such as the case of the Homestake Mine in Lead, South Dakota, which has operated continuously since 1877 and is continuing to increase its operations, and opening new gold mines, often in very disturbing locations, such as the proposed, and for now postponed, New World Mine, whose proposed location is about 2.5 miles from the border of Yellowstone National Park, near Cooke City, Montana.

This sentence contains too much information. For that reason, most of us would suggest breaking the sentence into two or perhaps three sentences, and our edit would serve the document because the revision would be easier for the audience to comprehend.

However, I often run across edits that do not serve the document. Consider the following sentences:

> The same nutrients that make manure a valuable fertilizer also make it a water pollutant. In lakes and streams, these nutrients cause algal blooms, kill fish, and make the water unsafe for swimming and drinking.

On similar sentences, I have witnessed editors make incorrect form edits: changing the "that" to a "which" and placing a comma after "fertilizer." These errors could be attributed to those editors not knowing these two rules of usage and punctuation.

I also have witnessed editors removing the comma after "streams" (the comma is optional) and removing the comma after "fish" (also optional, but recommended). Here the editors have made form edits that could be explained, but were unnecessary. Difficult to explain, though, is the following edit for style:

> The same nutrients that make manure a valuable fertilizer also make it a water pollutant. These nutrients, in lakes and streams, cause algal blooms, kill fish, and make the water unsafe for swimming and drinking.

In this style edit, the editor has rearranged the prepositional phrase "in lakes and streams," which was fine in its original location. The problem with such an edit is that it confuses the author, who is not sure why the change was made. Moreover, this preference edit weakens the power of a universal edit such as breaking up the huge sentence about the mines.

Often, preference edits arise in documents that are well written. Editing such documents should be a task that is welcomed. Yet some people mistakenly believe that they have to find mistakes to show everyone that they have, in fact, edited the piece. Insecurity spawns this misconception. In editing a paper that is well done, you often have to work to convince other editors that the document is strong. Convincing others that a document is strong usually requires as much work as convincing others that it is weak. Also, if you cannot identify what is strong in a piece of writing, then perhaps that piece of writing is not strong. Perhaps the document does not make and defend important assertions. Perhaps the document wallows in the abstract. If so, then the document has problems that you have not realized.

How to Phrase a Stylistic Edit. As with content edits, anchoring generalities with convincing examples is important in a stylistic edit. For instance, one reviewer of a recent journal submission wrote that the writing was "poor." The reviewer gave no example—just the statement that the writing was "poor." When the author asked for clarification through the journal's editor, the reviewer wrote back that the author had used the verb "show" instead of "demonstrate." While the reviewer finally provided an example, the example was not particularly convincing. Even H.W. Fowler's tome, *Modern English Usage* [1965], does not distinguish between these two words. Now, if there is a clear distinction between the two words, the reviewer should have not only stated the distinction, but also explained why this distinction was large enough to warrant the label "poor writing" on the paper. Because of the weak case made by the reviewer, both the author and the journal editor discounted this reviewer's assessment.

Editing for Form

Editing for form calls upon you to assess whether the grammar, punctuation, usage, spelling, and format are appropriate for the audience, purpose, and occasion. Although form edits appear to address relatively minor aspects of the writing, they often cause the most discord between editors and authors. Why is that so? One reason is that this type of edit occurs near the document's completion when people are usually tired of the document and want it to be off their desks.

Another reason that edits for form cause discord is that while most editors and authors accept variety in questions of style, they expect universality in questions of form. Unfortunately, because English is a blend of languages (Anglo-Saxon, Latin, Greek, French, German, Spanish, and so on), it is a language of exceptions. The next chapter gives an overview as to how gray areas have arisen in form. Moreover, the Appendix goes a step further by examining one hundred gray issues that cause contention among editors and authors in business, engineering, and science. The intent in both these examinations is not to help you decide who was the victor about the last question of form in your place of work, but to help you and your colleagues find a form for your writing upon which you can agree.

Of all the differences in form, the differences in format are easiest to explain. Format is the typography and layout of a document, and the choices for format vary widely from institution to institution. While IBM might choose one typeface for the text of reports, Dow Chemical might choose another. When editing the format of a document, having a simple checklist is helpful. Such a list ensures that you consider all those points that you want to consider. Figure 2-4 presents a list of common variables in a typical format. The actual format choice,

---

Checklist for Format

Typefaces

Text	Footnotes
Major headings	Figure captions
Subheadings	Table headings
Sub-subheadings	Figure call-outs

Layout

Margins	Paragraph indents
Line spacing	Paragraph spacing
Position of major headings	Page numbers in text
Position of subheadings	Page numbers in front matter
Position of sub-subheadings	Page numbers in back matter

Illustrations

Illustration names in text	Placement of illustrations
Illustration names in back matter	Size of illustrations

References

Reference listings in the text	Reference citations at end

Figure 2-4. Variables that you should consider in checking the format of a document.

such as 12 point Times New Roman for the text type, would depend on the typography and layout specified by the institution or publication.

For other aspects of form (grammar, punctuation, usage, and spelling), having a hierarchy rather than a checklist serves editors better. Figure 2-5 presents my own hierarchy for one issue of usage: commonly confused word pairs. In this hierarchy, I differentiate between the severity of the usage error. In my view, major usage errors such as confusing *affect* with *effect* would unsettle readers to the point of those readers losing confidence in the author. In other words, the mistake would raise questions about the education of the author: How much does this author read? On the other extreme, minor errors such as using *compare to* instead of *compare with* would not be noticed by many readers. Many errors fall in between. Some of these such as using *a* when *an* is appropriate will distract many readers, but will not affect the interpretation. Others such as confusing *enormity* with *enormousness* could dramatically alter the meaning of a sentence, although only a few readers might be aware of the difference in meaning. Figure 2-6 presents a similar hierarchy not only for usage, but for all aspects of mechanics: grammar, punctuation, usage, and spelling.

What is the value of such a hierarchy? Should not an editor correct every error in a document? When editing a long document, such as a major proposal or dissertation, you probably will not have the energy to enforce every error of form that you notice. In some cases, so many er-

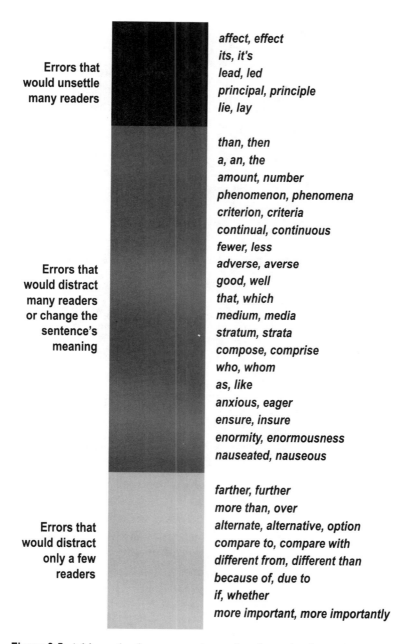

Figure 2-5. A hierarchy for commonly confused word pairs (an issue of usage) in professional documents. A discussion of each word pair appears in the Appendix.

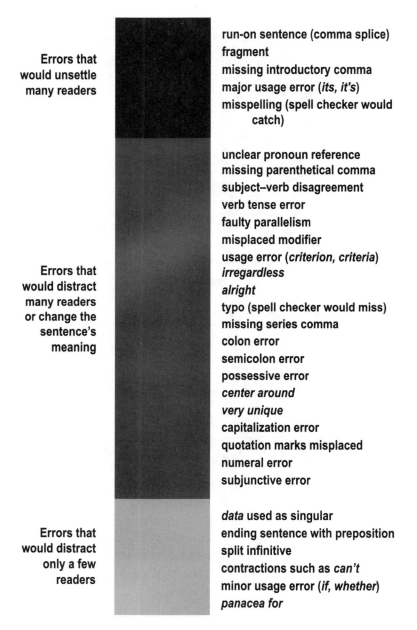

Errors that would unsettle many readers

run-on sentence (comma splice)
fragment
missing introductory comma
major usage error (*its, it's*)
misspelling (spell checker would catch)

Errors that would distract many readers or change the sentence's meaning

unclear pronoun reference
missing parenthetical comma
subject–verb disagreement
verb tense error
faulty parallelism
misplaced modifier
usage error (*criterion, criteria*)
irregardless
alright
typo (spell checker would miss)
missing series comma
colon error
semicolon error
possessive error
center around
very unique
capitalization error
quotation marks misplaced
numeral error
subjunctive error

Errors that would distract only a few readers

data used as singular
ending sentence with preposition
split infinitive
contractions such as *can't*
minor usage error (*if, whether*)
panacea for

Figure 2-6. A hierarchy for grammar, punctuation, usage, and spelling errors in a professional document. A discussion of each listing appears in the Appendix.

rors might exist that addressing them all would mean missing the document's deadline. In other cases, the author would not have enough energy to correct all the form errors in the document. In still other cases, marking every single error would produce so many notations on the page that the author would undoubtedly miss some (and, likely as not, the most important ones). For that reason, having a hierarchy helps you decide where you are going to draw the line.

Chapter 3

When the Rules Are Gray

The English speaking world may be divided into (1) those who neither know nor care what a split infinitive is; (2) those who do not know, but care very much; (3) those who know and condemn; (4) those who know and approve; and (5) those who know and distinguish. Those who neither know nor care are the vast majority and are a happy folk, to be envied by most of the minority classes.

H.W. Fowler

One hot California afternoon, a department manager phoned and asked me to come to his office. This manager, with whom I jogged occasionally and whose work I respected, closed the phone call in an unusual way, "Don't speak to anyone. Just come directly here." As soon as I entered his office, I knew that something was wrong. Across the room from the department manager was my supervisor. She stood in one corner, her lips drawn, her cheeks tense, her eyes wide and fierce.

"Don't look at her," the department manager said. "Don't even look at me. Just look at the first two sentences of this brochure." Spread on the table in front of me were the galleys of a brochure on supercomputers. Both my supervisor and the manager had been working on this brochure, the department manager being the lead writer and my supervisor serving, at least in her mind, as an editor. The first two sentences read as follows:

> The concepts of "capacity" and "capability" are important to our discussion of supercomputers. We will illustrate these concepts using __ historical analogy.

"You notice that a word is missing," the manager said. "We disagree on what that word should be, and we'd like you to settle the question. Should it be *a* or *an*?"

Surely this was a prank, I thought. My supervisor's expression, though, clearly revealed that it was not. Stalling for time, I stared at the page. My internal ear said that "a historical" was correct, but I had long since learned not to trust my internal ear on important questions (I grew up in southern Appalachia, which is not known for its adherence to the accepted rules of grammar and usage). Moreover, my experience of settling arguments between authors and editors told me to remain silent. Much was invested by these two in this question, much more than a choice between two articles. Finally I said that I had a suspicion as to which article was correct, but would like to consult my sources.

The department manager offered his dictionary, a huge, weathered book with gilt-edged pages and a frayed red spine. Because the book was open to words beginning with *h*, I declined the offer. These two had already gone down that road, and without resolution.

Silently cursing my luck, I returned to my office. Upon consulting several of my books, including *The Chicago*

Manual of Style [1993], I learned that the *h* in "historical" once was silent, like the *h* in "hour" or "heir." For that reason, years ago, people wrote "an historical." However, as the pronunciation of "historical" changed to an aspirated *h*, so did the article before it. At present, English calls for writing "a historical."

Returning to the department manager's office, I presented the history of this word without foreshadowing my conclusion. I acknowledged the use of *an historical* in the nineteenth century, before discussing the change in pronunciation. In stating my conclusion, I referred to the latest edition of *The Chicago Manual of Style*, but even as the axe fell, I tried to give the department manager, who had insisted upon "an historical," a graceful out by repeating that the English language is in flux and that it is difficult to keep up with all the changes.

I wish that I could report that peace was made and that work on the brochure proceeded smoothly. I cannot. Despite my best efforts, the author–editor relationship ended coldly, with the author doing the brochure his way (and claiming, by the way, that he "didn't give a damn for the way they did things in Chicago"). Interestingly, in the final version of that brochure the department manager used neither *a* nor *an* before "historical," circumventing the issue by writing "with historical analogy."

Although the story does not have a happy ending, it does provide insight into a difficult part of editing—the handling of gray rules. Three principles should guide you in approaching the gray rules of English.

Principle 1: The English language is not constant with respect to time.

Principle 2: The English language is not constant with respect to position.

Principle 3: The relative importance of rules in the English language is not constant with respect to person.

Gray with Respect to Time

As indicated in the story of "a historical" and "an historical," aspects of our language change with time. These changes are not as clear-cut as in other languages. German, for instance, has recently undergone a change in the spelling of many words. For instance, *Busineß* has become *Business*, *Floppy disk* has become *Floppydisk*, and *Schmuckblattelegramm* has become *Schmuckblatttelegramm* (three *t*'s). These changes were agreed upon by a committee, the rules were printed in a special section of the newspaper ["neue Rechtschreibung," 1997], and a date was set for when the rules would apply (1 August 1998). Although protests caused revisions to some of these proposed changes, the process for rule changes was in the open, and the timetable was clear.

English is not so orderly (*ordentlich*, as the Germans would say). We do not have such an authoritative committee. In the United States, we often look at what is done in the *New York Times* or the *Wall Street Journal*. Even here, we have to be careful. For many years, the *New York Times* was adamant about using *who* for the subjects of clauses and *whom* for objects in clauses, even when that meant placing *whom* as the first word of a sentence or title. One Sunday, though, William Safire [1997] declared in his "On Language" column that using *whom* to begin a sentence had become outmoded. After that column, the *Times* no longer had sentences such as "Whom will you support?" It was now "Who will you support?" (Note that Safire says that *For Whom the Bell Tolls* is still proper because *whom* is not the first word in that title.) Even though you might follow the lead of William Safire in this usage, you have to realize that no consensus has been reached. For instance, both the *Wall Street Journal* and *US News & World Report* still begin sentences with *whom*.

Several word pairs similar to *who* and *whom* are in flux, including *comprise* and *compose*, *farther* and *further*, and *nauseated* and *nauseous*. Why do such words change their meanings? Consider the case of *nauseated* and *nauseous*. Years ago, the word *nauseous* had only the one meaning of producing sickness or queasiness ("The odors were nauseous"), while the past participle *nauseated* provided the meaning of feeling sick to the stomach ("Only a few hours after the treatment, many patients became nauseated"). However, people, out of ignorance or laziness, began using *nauseous* when *nauseated* was called for ("Chemotherapy makes many patients nauseous"). Much as viruses spread, so does misuse in language until in this case the instances of misuse have outnumbered the instances of correct usage. Dictionaries, which report the way people use words, began including this secondary definition for *nauseous*. Granted, this secondary definition is labeled as colloquial, but with time and with use by more people and writers, the label colloquial might be dropped. When that occurs, the language will have evolved such that the misuse will have become accepted usage.

Gray with Respect to Position

The second principle, namely that the English language is not constant with respect to position, is even trickier than the first. For instance, should you write the years between 1990 and 1999 as the *1990's* or the *1990s*? Or should you place end quotation marks inside or outside of periods? Both of these questions strike a gray area of punctuation or usage for which the solution depends on where you are.

For instance, the *New York Times* writes the years between 1990 and 1999 as the *1990's*, but *Chemical and Engineering News* writes it as the *1990s*. Interestingly, up until the mid-1980s, *Chemical and Engineering News* wrote it the other way. Here the answer to the question depends upon which publication or institution you are editing for. Answered in this way are many writing questions, including questions of format (such as how to reference citations) and style (such as whether to use the first person *I* or *we*).

Other writing questions, such as whether to place end

quotation marks inside or outside of periods, depend upon where you are publishing. In the United States, you place end quotation marks outside the period. In Great Britain, though, you place the quotation marks inside (unless the period is part of the quotation).

Because of these differences, most publications and institutions either create or follow a style manual. The term "style manual" is actually a misnomer because the manual handles not only gray-area questions of style but also gray-area issues of format, grammar, punctuation, spelling, and usage. The Appendix of this book presents a style manual of sorts for professional writing. You should *not* consider the offerings in this manual as gospel. Although I present arguments for each choice, you might very well have good reasons, such as historical convention at your institution, for disagreeing. Still, the Appendix identifies controversial issues so that you can anticipate and address these gray-rule predicaments.

Gray with Respect to Person

A professor who taught a design class swung by my office one day to ask whether I had impressed upon the students the importance of good writing.

"I have tried," I answered.

"Yes, but your students are making some serious mistakes."

"Such as?"

"For one thing, they are splitting infinitives. For another, they're using contractions. And I've caught them numerous times ending sentences with prepositions."

Now, in my fifteen years of teaching, I have seen students make many mistakes, but with regard to importance, these three are not even on my list. Topping my list are other questions: Are the students writing complete sentences? Are the meanings of those sentences clear? Do those sentences convey the content precisely?

Next to capital crimes such as imprecision and ambiguity, the cases of split infinitives, contractions, and prepositions at the ends of sentences do not even warrant the label "misdemeanors." I asked this professor whether he made it clear to his students up front that he would not tolerate violations of these rules. Yes, he said. Then I asked this professor whether he had explained why these rules were so important. To this question, the professor had no answer except that he had always been taught they were important.

"When you give them a logical reason to follow those rules, they will follow those rules. And when you explain to me why those rules are as important as the ones I teach, I will teach those rules."

This story illustrates the third principle of gray-area rules, namely that each of us has a different ranking of importance for the rules of English. Don't get me wrong: I respect the professor's desire for his students to write well. It is just that I disagree with his ranking of what is important in strong writing, and if he intends to impose his ranking on others, then he should justify that ranking.

How did his ranking come about? It probably arose from the influence of his writing teachers. In addition to teaching us a wealth of traits and rules for good writing, writing teachers influence us about which traits and rules are important. Interestingly, the rules that this professor remembered are some of the easiest to apply in an edit. For instance, we can unequivocally state when an infinitive has been split, when a contraction occurs, and when a preposition ends a sentence. Granted, while avoiding these occurrences will improve the writing in some instances, in other instances avoiding them will make the writing needlessly complex. For example, consider Sir Winston Churchill's sarcastic reply to someone who chastised him for ending a sentence with a preposition: "My humblest apologies. Ending a sentence with a preposition is something up with which I will not put."

Because each of us has a different hierarchy for the importance of rules, we should be sensitive to what our own hierarchies are and why we have them. In particular, we should be able to justify our pet peeves: those rules that are not universally applied or are not considered as important by others. Here, I am not talking about rules such as striving for precision or avoiding ambiguities — these rules are at the top of every editor's hierarchy. Rather, I am talking about idiosyncratic rules that you desire to have followed, even though many other editors do not. For instance, some editors cringe any time that *comprise* is used as a synonym for *compose*. For these editors, the word *comprise* has only the one meaning "to include." Therefore, the whole comprises the parts, and the phrase *is comprised of* makes no sense. However, if you examine the use of *comprise* in most documents, you will find it misused more often than not. Such a rule then, when strictly enforced by an editor, falls within my definition of pet peeves.

Given below are my pet peeves and my explanations for holding them. Some of these pet peeves, such as not using *however* as a coordinating conjunction, are rules found in every writing handbook, but they are rules that I find particularly important and often broken. Other pet peeves such as the naked *this* are my own rules, and you will probably not find them in other writing handbooks. Still other pet peeves such as inserting the series comma are rules that writing handbooks disagree about, but upon which I take a strong stand.

Alley's Pet Peeves

naked *this* — avoid. To make a transition from one sentence to the next, many authors use a naked *this* ("*This* places an upper limit on the concentration of olefins"). Because the *this* stands alone, rather than points to a specific noun, it causes an ambiguity: Does the *this* refer to the last noun of the previous sentence, to the subject of the previous sentence, to the idea of the previous sentence, or in the case of some writers to none of the above? When used consistently to refer to the idea of the previous sentence, such usage is acceptable, but consistency must be maintained.

bureaucratic nouns — avoid. Each of us has a list of words that we find pretentious. These words appear to have been chosen not to inform or to persuade the audience, but to impress the audience. Several nouns top my list: *facilitation* (use "helping," "causing," or "bringing about"), *implementation* (use "carrying out"), *operationability* (rewrite the sentence using "can operate"), *prioritization* (use "ranking"), and *utilization* (use "use").

however to join two independent clauses — avoid. The word *however* is not a coordinating conjunction. Many people mistakenly use *however* (as well as *therefore* and *otherwise*) as a coordinating conjunction to join two independent clauses: "The chamber exploded, however, no one was hurt." This mistake, which is called a run-on sentence or comma splice, is serious because it indicates that the writer does not understand what constitutes a sentence. The following are possible solutions:

The chamber exploded, but no one was hurt.

Although the chamber exploded, no one was hurt.

The chamber exploded. However, no one was hurt.

Note that it is now acceptable to begin a sentence with "however." Years ago, for some reason, the practice was frowned upon.

series comma — in punctuating a series of three or more items, follow the conservative advice of William Strunk [1918] and place a comma after each item except the last. For example, write "carbon, hydrogen, and oxygen." While leaving out the last comma in this list would not confuse the audience, many professional papers have at least one list in which the last comma is crucial to understanding — for example, "production, marketing, and research and development." Keeping the last comma makes your writing consistent and instills reader confidence when the lists become complicated: "lakes, rivers, estuaries, and man-made bodies, such as impoundments, drainage ditches, and canals."

needless abbreviations — avoid. Professional writing is complex enough as it is without needless abbreviations that make the writing appear even more complex and that sap strength from the most powerful piece of punctuation, the period. The following are abbreviations to avoid and possible words to substitute (in parentheses): *i.e.* (that is), *e.g.* (for example), *fig.* (figure), and *vs.* (versus).

exclamation point — avoid. The overuse of this punctuation in *Dick and Jane* readers has poisoned its use in professional writing.

This third principle of recognizing that each of us has a different hierarchy of gray rules is important because we often do not edit alone, and when editors indiscriminately impose their pet peeves on authors, those authors become confused.

Chapter 4

Common Editing Situations

Edit ruthlessly. Somebody ~~has~~ said that words are ~~a lot~~ like inflated money—the more ~~of them that~~ you use, the less each one ~~of them~~ is worth.

Malcolm Forbes

The word processing program altered what you had just edited. Without asking or prompting, the program simply reformatted a sentence that you had just added. What was the first sentence of a new paragraph is now the fourth item of a list. You quickly change this item back to a sentence, but the word processing program even more quickly makes the sentence an item of the list again.

You are beyond frustration. Just a while ago, for more than twenty minutes, you struggled in vain to modify that same list from having numbers followed by periods to having the numbers followed by right parentheses:

1.	→	1)
2.	→	2)
3.	→	3)

A pet peeve of yours is that periods should serve only one function—to end sentences. Unfortunately, whenever you replaced the period with a right parenthesis, the program overrode your edit to insert both pieces of punctuation:

    1.)
    2.)
    3.)

In the end, you decided that a period following the number was a lesser evil than redundant punctuation.

Working with this computer program is usually not a problem for you, but the proposal you are editing uses a new version of the program. You consider just printing out the original version of the proposal, editing it on paper, and then having your secretary, who is a whiz with this program, keystroke in the changes. Unfortunately, it is Saturday, and the proposal team expects your edited version early on Monday morning. You scroll through the legion of topics in the online help and wonder how many people in the world are having the same problem.

   '   Managers, scientists, and engineers often find themselves in one of four editing situations: reviewing a document, copyediting a document on paper, copyediting a document on the computer, and proofreading a document. This chapter focuses on the major hurdles of each situation and offers strategies for overcoming those hurdles. For each of these situations, you have to consider more than just one of the three editing perspectives of content, style, or form. For instance, a review, which occurs early in the publication process, usually focuses both on content and on big-picture issues of style such as organization and depth. Moreover, a proof, which occurs late in the editing process, usually addresses both form and sentence-level aspects of style and content.

Although this chapter offers editing strategies for each situation, you should understand that the strategy you invoke for a document also depends on the overall editing process. For instance, in reviewing a document that will later have a detailed copyedit , you have the luxury of not worrying about sentence-level details. Here you can focus on the big picture (the content and organization). However, in reviewing a document that does not have a detailed copyedit stage, you should also address suggestions at the sentence level. One way to do so is to attach a list of sentence-level suggestions to your big-picture assessment.

Writing a Review

A review is an overall sweep of a document. The purpose of this sweep varies a great deal. For instance, a review of a journal submission assesses whether the journal should publish that submission. In another case, an in-house review of a company proposal assesses whether the authors are on the proper track with that proposal. In general, a review focuses on the content of the document and overall stylistic issues such as organization and depth. Because a review occurs in the early stages of the publication process, not as much energy is spent on sentence-level issues of style and form because these issues could disappear as sections are cut or heavily revised.

A review not only helps the journal, publisher, or institution decide whether the document is worthy of publication, but also informs the author of the overall strengths and weaknesses of the document so that the author can improve that document. Given in Figure 4-1 are sample criteria for a review of a journal paper.

Often the actual review comments are not written on the document being edited, but on separate sheets of paper. For that reason, a review should be well organized and deliver proper emphasis. Another way of looking at this piece of advice is that the characteristics of a well-crafted review are also the characteristics of a well-crafted content edit, which was discussed in Chapter 2. For that reason, a review should clarify your overall stand on the

---

Checklist for Reviewers
Is the paper within the scope of the journal?
Is there a significant amount of new work in the paper?
Is the style acceptable?
Does the paper contain errors of fact or logic?
Is any of the material superfluous?
Should any material be transferred to appendices?
Are the illustrations necessary, informative, and sufficient?
Are the references adequate?
Is the title a brief and accurate indication of the contents?
Is the abstract a fair and concise summary of the paper?
Does the notation conform to SI Units?
If the paper needs drastic revision, should another author be
    recruited?

Figure 4-1. Criteria for review of papers submitted to the *Journal of Turbomachinery* [ASME, 1998]. Most questions pertain to content.

document and should assign a weight to the importance of the criticisms.

Two examples of reviews are provided in Figures 4-2 and 4-3. These examples are reviews of different journal papers by the same reviewer. In the first example, the reviewer recommended acceptance of the paper for publication, while in the second example, she did not. One thing important to pick up from these examples is the structure. In each review, the reviewer began with an overall assessment of the paper. In other words, by the end of the first paragraph, the reviewer made it clear to the author and to the journal editor what her stand was with respect to publication.

Also, in each review, the reviewer clearly established a hierarchy for the criticisms. In establishing these hierarchies, the reviewer limited each review to two or three main points. Because this publication process did not include a detailed copyedit, the reviewer felt compelled to mention sentence-level criticisms. How did she do that and keep the emphasis on her two or three main points? In the first review, in which she had five major criticisms, she used paragraph breaks to show that three of the criticisms were more important than the remaining two. In doing so, the reviewer made sure that the most important edits were not passed over. After all, not all edits are equal in importance. In the second review, because there were too many minor points to incorporate into a paragraph on the main page, she listed those points on a separate sheet. Notice that a long list of sentence-level con-

Review of "Influence of Heat Conduction on the Temperature Distribution in Turbine Blades"

The reviewed paper presents an analysis to help turbine designers assess the temperature variations occurring along a gas turbine blade. Given the importance and thoroughness of the work, I recommend this paper for publication. However, the following items should be clarified beforehand:

1) One of the assumptions made throughout this paper is that the heat transfer coefficients on the inside of the gas turbine blade are at a constant value h_i. The literature, however, shows that this value can vary. For that reason, the authors should state what this variation of h_i is, based on the literature, and how that variation affects the solutions.

2) The heat transfer coefficients given in Figure 2 are much higher than what is found in the literature for turbine blade heat transfer at a turbulence intensity of 10 percent. I ask that the authors refer to a recent paper by Hoffs, Drost, and Bolcs (ASME Paper No. 96-GT-169). Although the Reynolds number in this referenced paper (320,000) is much higher than the Reynolds number of the paper reviewed here, the heat transfer coefficients are 10 times lower than the coefficients of the reviewed paper, even though the turbulence levels are the same. I suggest that the authors check their conversions from Stanton number to the heat transfer coefficients and, if those conversions are correct, discuss why their heat transfer coefficients are so high.

3) Another assumption made by the authors is that the convective cooling in the film-cooling hole can be neglected. In actual cooling of gas turbine blades, the cooling that occurs in the cooling holes accounts for 45 percent of the heat removed. Thus, near the cooling hole the dominant heat transfer may be the heat conducted to the cooling hole. How might the authors consider this effect in their analysis?

Two minor points should also be addressed. First, Figure 3 does not have the correct nomenclature: T_w should be T_{wo}, and ΔT_w should be ΔT_{wo}. Second, the authors should reconsider the term "ridges," which implies a physical protuberance. I suggest using "rises" or "declines," depending on the situation.

Figure 4-2. Sample review of a journal paper in which the reviewer recommends publication. Most of the edits in this sample are content edits.

Review of "Heat Transfer Using Infrared Thermography: Error Estimation and Application"

The reviewed paper describes how to correlate the radiation temperature and the true surface temperature when using an infrared camera. In addition, this paper presents an error analysis when using an infrared camera for quantitative forced and free convective measurements of heat transfer. Although the topic of this paper is clear, the emphasis of this paper is not. For that reason, I cannot recommend it for publication.

If the emphasis of this paper is that the authors have proven that infrared thermography can be used to determine forced and free convection correlations in heat transfer, then the paper does not warrant publication because such quantitative measurements have already been published. One example for forced convection is Scherer and others [1991], and one example for free convection is Heng and Black [1991]. Both of these studies include uncertainty estimates. If the emphasis is to establish the best correlation for determining heat transfer coefficients, this paper fails in that only one data set (one Reynolds number range) is compared with only one correlation for forced convection.

If the emphasis is error analysis, then some important quantities have to be added to the authors' discussion. For instance, because the thermocouples are imbedded 0.5 mm below the top surface, the authors should discuss the analysis of differences between the true surface temperature and the temperature sensed by the thermocouple. For this analysis, the authors should consider a two-dimensional finite element analysis. Also, not enough information is given so that readers can evaluate the uncertainty analysis. For instance, the authors don't give the raw uncertainties of certain quantities such as the wall heat flux. The authors don't discuss how voltage and current are measured (which might reveal errors in the resistance). Finally, the authors don't mention the time that the freestream temperature is maintained at a constant temperature relative to the thermal time constant of the test plate.

The next page lists other concerns about the paper and gives citations to the references mentioned here.

Figure 4-3. Sample review of a journal paper in which the reviewer does not recommend publication. Most of the edits in this sample are content edits.

cerns, unlike such a list of big-picture concerns, does not undercut the emphasis. The reason is that the author can look at each sentence-level concern individually as he or she revises the manuscript.

Finally, notice that the reviewer worked just as hard in the review for the paper she recommended accepting as in the one she recommended not accepting. While the reviewer felt that neither paper was perfect, she believed that the weaknesses of the first one could be addressed without an overhaul of the work.

Performing a Copyedit on Paper

A copyedit, often called a line edit, is a sentence-by-sentence edit of a document that prepares the document for publication. While a review occurs relatively early in the publication process, a copyedit occurs during the later stages — after the overall content and structure of the document have been accepted. Because this edit occurs in the later stages, the focus is on sentence-level aspects of style and form. In a copyedit, you make marks line by line throughout the document. Because you are editing at the paragraph and sentence levels, you make your marks on the copy. Traditionally, these marks have been done with blue pencils. One reason for you to use a pencil is that the lead allows you the opportunity to erase, which is helpful because in copyedits you often go back and forth with how to reword a sentence. An advantage of using a colored pencil is that the color makes the marks stand out.

For copyedits, a shorthand convention has arisen that is worth learning. At the core of the convention is a set of marks, the most important of which are shown in Figure 4-4. Note that you place some of these marks within the text and some in the margin. Also note that where you have more than one copyedit per line, you use a slash (/) to separate each mark. Consider an example:

Some kinds ∧ turtles ag ∧ so slowly that many *of* # / *e*
scientists question whether they age at all.

In this example, the marks indicate that you insert both the word "of" and a space where the first caret appears

Common Editing Marks

∧	insert with caret		⌀	delete
cap	make uppercase		⍧	transpose
lc	Make lowercase		*stet*	let it stand
¶	new paragraph		#	add space
⫯	no new paragraph		⌣	close space
⊙	period		⌃	comma
⊙	semicolon		⊙	colon
╪M	em-dash (—)		╪N	en-dash (minus sign)
⊖	hyphen: the xray laser		⌄	apostrophe
⌄⌄	quotation marks		*italics*	italics
bf	boldface		*rom*	roman (normal)

Figure 4-4. Common editing marks. These marks appear either within the text or in the margins. Although these marks are fine for both copyedits and proofs, professional editors use a larger set of marks, some of which are different for copyedits and proofs.

and that you insert the letter *e* where the second caret appears. Note that whenever you place a mark in the text, you should place a corresponding mark in the margin to signal the author that you have suggested a change.

A second aspect of the convention for copyediting is that you encircle comments or questions to the author to distinguish those from letters and words that the author is to add. Finally, you use footnotes at the bottom of the page for longer comments. An example page from a copyedit appears in Figure 4-5.

Performing a Copyedit Online

Advances in computing have made it convenient in many situations to perform copyediting online (on the computer). An example would be editing a proposal on the Fastlane system of the National Science Foundation. In this system, all the proposal's sections (summary, project description, biographies, budget, and so forth) are placed onto the World Wide Web with access given only to those editing the proposal. Editing then becomes a matter of logging on and reworking the material—a system quite convenient, especially when the editors are scattered across the country.

Editing online has become much more sophisticated that just passing a floppy disk around the office. For instance, some word processing programs not only show the edited version of a document but also identify what changes have been made. Figure 4-6 shows a page from a

The R.M.S. Titanic, a ship once considered unsinkable, sank on the night of April 14, 1912. designs of the ship had estimated it *cap* / *that* would take one to three days for the Titanic to sink even under the worst conditions. Yet on ∧ its maiden voyage the Titanic sank in less than three hours after colliding with an iceberg. What caused the Titanic to sink so quickly?

One cause was a flaw in the design of the *au** bulkheads. Bulkheads are large walls erected inside a ship hull to partition it into compart- *#* ments. The bulkheads of the Titanic had two major problems: (1) the bulkheads were too short [Brander, 1995], and (2) the bulkheads were not waterprofed on top[Gannon, 1995]. *o / #* After the ship struck the iceberg water rushed ∧ in, filling the front five compartments. the *cap* added weight of this water caused the bow of the ship to sink deeper. Then water spilled over into the remaining compartments, eventually causing the Titanic to founder.

---

au*: should you not discuss the material flaws of the ship first, since the water would not have even entered the ship if the steel had met specifications?

Figure 4-5. Page that has been line edited. Note that messages to the author (au) are either circled in the margin or placed in footnotes at the bottom of the page.

The R.M.S. Titanic, a ship once considered
unsinkable, sank on the night of April 14, 1912.
Ddesigners of the ship had estimated that it
would take one to three days for the Titanic to
sink, even under the worst conditions. Yet on its
maiden voyage the Titanic sank in less than
three hours after colliding with an iceberg. What
caused the Titanic to sink so quickly?

One cause was a flaw in the design of the
bulkheads. Bulkheads are large walls erected
inside a ship's hull to partition it into compartments. The bulkheads of the Titanic had two
major problems: (1) the bulkheads were too
short [Brander, 1995], and (2) the bulkheads
were not waterproofed on top [Gannon, 1995].
After the ship struck the iceberg, water rushed
in, filling the front five compartments. Tthe
added weight of this water caused the bow of
the ship to sink deeper. Then water spilled over
into the remaining compartments, eventually
causing the Titanic to founder.

*Should you not discuss the material flaws of the ship
first, since the water would not have even entered the ship
if the steel had met specifications?

Figure 4-6. Text from Figure 4-5 that has been copyedited online. Note
that the inserted text is underlined, and the deleted text has been
struck through. The general comment has been inserted as a separate window below the paragraph to which it pertains.

document that has been edited online. The underlined characters have been added by the editor, and the strike-through lines indicate the characters that the editor deleted. On the computer screen, many programs offer the option of placing edits in different colors so that you can distinguish the edits of multiple editors.

Inherent problems exist, though, with online editing. One problem occurs because of the differences between computer software and hardware that authors and editors use. For instance, if you are unaccustomed to the program LaTeX, editing a document in that program poses a serious challenge. Even if all editors are familiar with the software program, editing online can be difficult when the author uses a version of that program different from the one to which the editors are accustomed. Different versions of the same program often have changes that can stymie an editor. Besides differences in software, differences in hardware can cause problems for online editing. For instance, using a PC to edit a document that was originally created on a Macintosh risks all sorts of errors even when the software program is the same version. Common errors include alterations in tab spacings, typefaces, and illustrations.

With online editing, another problem (which might appear to be an advantage) is that adding and deleting text online is easy. With a simple highlight and cut, you can erase an entire paragraph or section. The problem is that online additions and deletions of text are so easy that editors are more likely to make them. In a sign-off process with multiple editors, this ease of making changes can bring about the inclusion of many unnecessary changes, thus creating a visual mess on the screen that makes it difficult for the author and other editors to decipher what changes have been made and who made them.

Yet another problem with online editing is a problem encountered any time you incorporate new technology into the publication process: You have to learn the minefields. These minefields go beyond the discomfort and uncertainty that arise from trying something new. For instance, while incorporating online edits into a journal on the World Wide Web, we encountered a problem with the word-processed files that we had edited online. Because we had failed to clear the memory of the word-processing program after our online edits, the program retained the original wording in a masked form. When we saved the articles as text documents to place them into html (the language of the World Wide Web), all the original text surfaced. What resulted was chaos—all the articles had to be copyedited again, but this time on paper.

Granted, such a minefield could have been easily circumvented had we been aware of its existence. However, it is difficult to anticipate every minefield the first time that you incorporate new technology in the publication of a document. The lesson to be learned here is not to avoid online editing or other innovations in editing, but to test those innovations on a small scale so that you learn the minefields without too much loss of blood.

Proofreading

A proof is a final pass over a document to rid the document of unwanted errors. By the time a document reaches the proofreading stage, the document should have passed through a review and copyedit so that comments regarding content and style are unnecessary. In reality, this situation does not exist. One reason is that many production schedules do not include a formal review and copyedit. Another reason is that even after the best review and copyedit the document has not reached perfection in either content or style. In fact, sometimes clarifying a jumbled sentence on a copyedit exposes a flaw in logic that becomes apparent during the proof.

Nonetheless, in a proof, you want to make as few changes as possible related to style and content. Such changes at the end can introduce errors that do more harm than good. For instance, if an editor during the final proof of a report removes a sentence from page 3, the placement of headings, illustrations, and footnotes throughout the report can change. What can result are many more problems than the offending sentence would have caused. Moreover, keying in changes just before publication can cause glaring typographical errors that will undercut the authority of the author. As an editor, you have to balance the severity of the error against the inherent risk of other errors that correcting that error will bring. If the original error warrants the risk, you should advocate the change.

However, if the error is not actually an error, but a gray aspect of style or form, you should reconsider.

Because proofs occur at the end of the publication process, you have only so much time to devote to this stage. For that reason, you should spend your time and energy where it will do the most good. Remember: Not all mistakes are created equal. As shown back in Figure 2-6, errors of form vary greatly in their effect on readers. A misspelling that a spell-checker could catch is usually more egregious than a typo that a spell-checker could not identify. With the former, the audience realizes that the author did not even bother to perform a spell-check. The audience then wonders what else the author did not bother to do. Exceptions to this hierarchy do exist, of course. For instance, a single typo that alters the dollar amount in a sales contract could cause more grief and embarrassment than a host of misspellings.

In addition to the type of error, the position of an error affects how it is viewed. A mistake in a title, heading, first sentence, or illustration call-out stands out much more than the same mistake in the middle sentence of the middle paragraph of the middle section. In one recent textbook on editing (of all things), the first illustration had the call-out "language" misspelled. Since this illustration was the first one in the book and since the typeface for the misspelled word was significantly larger than the text type on the page, the mistake shouted at the reader. Figure 4-7 shows a hierarchy for positions in a document. The higher the document part is on the list, the more important is that part of the document to proof.

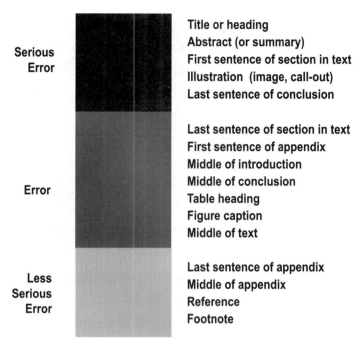

Figure 4-7. A proofreading hierarchy for the positions of items in a professional document. An error in a place with a higher profile is more serious than the same error in a portion with a lower profile.

Just because certain parts of a document have a lower profile than other parts does not mean that you can "dog" the proofreading of those less important parts; rather, it means that what time you spend proofreading you should allocate proportionately so that more important parts receive more attention.

Strangely enough, even though titles, headings, and illustrations receive more attention from the audience, these places are often overlooked by proofreaders. Perhaps the handsomeness of the type in the title or the image in the illustration lulls proofreaders into assuming that this portion of the document is above error. For example, in one newsletter that I edited for a prominent research laboratory, I unfortunately became complacent in the proofreading of a photograph. The photograph showed a row of scientists and managers at the laboratory welcoming a Nobel laureate chemist. The director of the laboratory, who was situated on the far left of the photo, had requested that he be cropped out of the photo, and I tried to oblige. However, the printer did not crop the photo exactly as I drew the marks, and one feature of the director remained in the photo—his nose. In the galley proofs I did not notice the nose, but once the newsletter came out, people around the laboratory did. "Hey, whose nose is that," some people asked. Soon came the replies, "I know whose nose that is." (The director had a prominent nose.) The blunder resulted in a mad dash to pick up copies from the desks around the laboratory and to stop the mailings. Unfortunately, the international mailings had already gone out.

Often with mistakes in illustrations, the error is not the focus of the illustration, but something in the background. In one of its issues, *Sports Illustrated* displayed a photograph of a student from UCLA in her dormitory room. The focus of the photograph was on the student, but the background of this picture included a button denigrating UCLA's archrival, USC. The button, which was in the maroon and gold of USC, contained a vulgarity that readers from USC, attuned to their school colors, did not miss.

Proofreading is difficult. Usually when we read a word, we do not examine every letter. That is because our mind sees the first couple of letters, recognizes the word by its shape and the context, and then moves on to the next word. How do you stop your mind from doing that? One way is to change the way you read. In one method of proofreading, for instance, you read the words aloud, which forces you to read slowly. This method is good for catching double words and missing words. Another method is to use rulers to cover the lines of text above and below so that you focus on the line at hand. While you may not have time to use these methods on entire documents, you might use them for those portions, such as titles and abstracts, that receive the most attention from readers. Try your hand at proofreading the paragraph in Figure 4-8. An edited version of this paragraph is shown in Figure 4-9.

When the *Titanic* struck the iceberg, two large gashes (one above and one below the waterline) ripped open the front five compartments. As the the cold Atlantic water filled these compartments, its weight pulled the bow of the *Titanic* deeper into the water. Because the bulkheads only extended about 10 feet above the waterline [Brander, 1995], water in the fifth compartment soon a spilled into sixth compartment. This additional weight pulled the bow down even farther. This pulling down of the bow continued until the stern of the ship, which was about 25 stories in length [Gannon, 1995] was lifted out of the water. Shortly therafter, the steel fractured in the middle of the ship.

Figure 4-8. A paragraph in need of proofreading. An edited version appears in Figure 4-9.

When the *Titanic* struck the iceberg, two large
gashes (one above and one below the waterline)
ripped open the front five compartments. As the
~~the~~cold Atlantic water filled these compartments,
its weight pulled the bow of the *Titanic* deeper into
the water. Because the bulkheads |only| extended|
about 10 feet above the waterline [Brander, 1995],
water in the fifth compartment soon a'spilled into
sixth compartment. This additional weight pulled
the bow down even farther. This pulling down of
the bow continued until the stern of the ship, which
was about 25 stories in length [Gannon, 1995] was
lifted out of the water. Shortly therafter, the steel
fractured in the middle of the ship.

Figure 4-9. A paragraph that has been proofread. Notice the diversity
of mistakes: double word, transposed words, extra word, missing
word, missing punctuation, and misspelled word.

Whichever of these methods you use, do not forget to
do a spell-check at the end. In typesetting a document
once, I failed to run a spell-check after moving the document from the word-processing program to the typesetting program. Excuses were plentiful: Two other people
besides me had proofread the document after it was typeset; I did not know how to run the spell-checker in the
page-making program; and the deadline for the document
to go to the printer had arrived. Those excuses paled,
though, against the errors that the document contained —
errors that the spell-check program would have caught.

Perhaps more important than the method of proofreading is the time, atmosphere, and mood in which you
proof. Proofreading in the bustle of the day with people
moving in and out of your office is nearly impossible. I

prefer to proofread in the serenity of the early morning —
door closed and no noise. I also accept that proofreading
is tiring work. Whenever I become tired and find myself
reading the words without really thinking about the
words, I do not hesitate to take a break. Proofreading is
not a glory task — it is a responsibility task. Most readers
do not notice when the proofreading has been done well,
but they certainly notice when it has not. Consider the
misplaced comma, on an international sales contract, that
cost one corporation an estimated $70 million ["Case,"
1999].

Reducing the Friction of Editing

People ask you for criticism, but they want only praise.
Somerset Maugham

On your business trip to Munich, you have three documents to edit: a report, a proposal, and a journal article. The authors of these documents vary widely in both writing skills and disposition. Daulton, the author of the report, is the most willing to accept suggestions — and with good reason. His writing is the least polished. Although he places his ideas in a logical order, he fails to make connections between those ideas. Sentences next to one another often do not relate to each other.

Leslie, who wrote the proposal, is both the best writer and the most defensive about changes. To say that Leslie thinks highly of her writing is an understatement. Even the first draft of her proposal was single-spaced. She expected no changes. John has the shortest document, and it is the one you dread the most. Of the three, John is the least attentive to detail. Moreover, although John is a decent writer, writing pains him. To have John rewrite a paragraph or even correct a misspelling in a document requires badgering.

You have a window seat for the flight, but no book, no magazine, and no desire to fritter two hours of your life on a Hollywood movie. All you have are the three documents before you.

Although editing presents many challenges, such as recognizing what is missing from a document or having the patience to copyedit a document fraught with language errors, the most challenging part of editing is working with authors, especially defensive authors. Somerset Maugham had it right—whenever an author hands you something to review, he or she secretly hopes that your response will be, "Don't change a word."

Nonetheless, not every author bristles every time you suggest changes—in fact, many appreciate the feedback on their work. Others who guard sentences on one report as if they were defending the Alamo are sometimes amenable to deeper changes on other documents. In other words, not all authors respond the same way to having their work edited, and the amount of defensiveness that each author holds for his or her writing often varies from document to document. Given this lack of uniform response, no single formula exists for removing the tension from the editing process. Still, much can be done to reduce the inherent tension that exists with editing.

Agreeing upon the Constraints

It is three o'clock in the morning, but your plane is still over the Atlantic. Although the movie has ended and most of the lights in the cabin are off, you are wide awake. Spread out before you is Daulton's report on the shapes of air holes for cooling turbine blades. You are not happy about being awake this late, but the dull roar from the combustion of fuel in the engines prevents you from sleeping. It is not the noise of the engines that keeps you awake, but how much you know about the engines. You know, for instance, that the combustion temperatures in the engines are so high that were it not for using the outside air as a coolant, the turbine blades would melt. At this morning's conference, in Munich, you will pay for your inability to sleep now, but since you are awake, you decide to make the most of the time.

Daulton's report reads essentially as a first draft. No more than a page into it, you begin to ignore the weak transitions between sentences, and focus on the content and structure. What Daulton says about the cooling holes is correct and the way he organizes the details is logical, but he does not understand the audience. For one thing, he does not emphasize the result that will interest his audience the most—namely, that the angle of the hole is just as important for cooling as the hole's shape. Moreover, his background section in the report's beginning is more than twenty pages, but that section contains information his primary audience already knows. For that reason, this section would be better placed in an appendix.

Agitated, you write down the word "audience" three times in the margin. Even if you were in your own bedroom, the night cool and silent, you would not be able to sleep now. Frustration has that effect on you.

In writing a document, certain constraints exist: the purpose of the document; the audience for the document; the format for the document; and the politics governing the document. Much friction occurs between editing managers and authors because an author will assume one set of constraints and the manager will assume another. Once I was brought in to work on a brochure that a manager had asked an engineer to draft. The draft was nothing that the manager had imagined. The manager had it in his head that the length of the brochure would be about eight pages and that the primary audience would be nontechnical. The engineer, on the other hand, had spent two intense weeks writing a forty-page document for a technical audience. In the end the engineer was bitter that most of the work he had done was for naught.

As an editing manager, you and your author should agree on the constraints early in the writing process. One good check is to define the constraints in a memo or e-mail. Moreover, on all outlines and drafts, the author should include a short description of the document's audience and purpose to remind all editors, as well as himself or herself, what those constraints are. While a spoken agreement about the constraints is good, a written agreement is incontrovertible.

Recognizing Your Own Idiosyncracies

It is Friday noon, *der Himmel ist klar*, and from the church spires of Munich you can see the Bavarian Alps. Although you would love to eat some *Wurst* at the outside market near the *Marienplatz* and then wander down to the *Deutsches Museum* to stroll through the exhibit on flight, you have forbidden yourself all travel pleasures until you finish editing Leslie's proposal. Of the three documents that you have brought on this trip, Leslie's is by far the best written. However, of the three people whose work you are editing, Leslie is by far the most temperamental. Whatever changes you suggest will have to withstand her scrutiny.

With Leslie's proposal, your principal criticisms do not concern the content — what she has to say is well considered and her analysis of the audience is dead on. Rather, most of your questions concern the way she phrases some of her points. Stylistically, Leslie is so ambitious in varying her sentence structures that you question whether she might be making mechanical errors. For instance, she uses the semicolon, a piece of punctuation that you tend to avoid, in ways you have not seen before.

Still, you have developed a strategy for handling Leslie, one that you used effectively on an earlier report of hers and one that you will use here. The strategy takes advantage of one of her character traits: her desire for perfection. So instead of asking her to change a sentence because you are not sure whether it is punctuated correctly, you simply raise the question whether the punctuation is correct. In fact, your edit of her proposal will consist of a series of questions, written in the margin and circled. *Correct use of semicolon? Sentence too long here?* You will give Leslie no commands, just questions, and because of her drive for perfection, she will check and recheck each one.

Each of us has strong likes and dislikes about writing, and many of these likes and dislikes are not universal, but have arisen because of our education and experience. For instance, the words *facilitate, utilization,* and *prioritize* make me cringe. Why? The first time that I heard those words was years ago when a salesman used them to try to bamboozle me into buying an inferior product. The idea of being suckered by such a ploy revolted me so much that I associated those words with him.

Chapter 3 discussed the importance of letting your authors know your pet peeves so that they are not surprised when you mark those aspects. One government manager took this point a step further by developing a program that flagged bureaucratic words that he did not want his staff to write. In this manager's division, when someone typed in *prioritization, operationability,* or *utilization,* the network sent that staff member a warning that the manager did not want this word to be used. While these measures might appear drastic, they did remove any doubt about where the manager stood on that aspect of style.

It is important not only that you know what your pet peeves are, but that you understand why you hold those peeves. By justifying your pet peeves, you force yourself to come to terms with why you hold those criticisms to be so important. If appropriate, you should share those pet peeves with those authors whose work you continually edit. While doing so invites the authors to challenge the validity of those pet peeves, you will find that the pet peeves that are well justified will withstand the challenge. Moreover, allowing others to critique your list can help you communicate better the precise issues of writing that disturb you.

Keeping the Writing on Schedule

Although you are eager to see your family again, you will miss your morning walks through the *Englisher Garten,* your one *Weißbier* at lunch, and the relaxed dinners with your German colleagues. At those dinners, the conversation focused on only one or two topics during the entire evening, each topic savored and explored in depth. You are proud that half of the conversation has been in German, although your German is not nearly as fluent (*fließend*) as your colleagues' English.

Now you are flying home. You have put off proofreading John's article until the flight home. Although John's article is the shortest of the three documents, it is the one that frightens you the most because your edit is the final pass over this document before publication. The audience will be large, which means that the risk for embarrassment is great. Moreover, of the three authors, John is the least attentive to detail. Worse yet, coaxing John to write a document is as difficult as coaxing a group of Germans at a bus stop to form a single line. That is why you have secured John's permission to make the changes online yourself. Otherwise, the proofed article would lie dormant on his desk.

In this edit, you will work with both a hard copy and a computer file copy—the hard copy to proof, and the computer file copy to make changes and to perform a spell-check, which you doubt John has done. During the proof, you are nervous that an embarrassing mistake will slip through. Your mood is a sharp contrast to the subdued spirits of those around you—everyone else relaxing on the long westward journey.

When a deadline approaches, the stress involved with editing increases exponentially because a document behind schedule often needs more work than there are hours in the day. Such was the case for an engineering professor who received a copy of a student's dissertation three weeks before that student was to graduate. This student had been a model student up to that point, but until that point had not submitted any writing to the professor. Although the engineering in the project was strong, the dissertation documenting the project was weak. The chapters required major reorganization; sentences were riddled with imprecision; and mistakes in grammar, punctuation, and usage abounded. While the student did have three weeks to make the writing passable, there was not nearly enough time to raise the document to the professor's standards. Given that, the professor was faced with two choices: allow the student to submit a dissertation that was merely satisfactory, or force the student to postpone graduation until the dissertation met the professor's standards. Complicating the decision was that the student (a new parent) already had a job lined up to begin as soon as the semester ended.

This professor's dilemma might have been avoided had the professor requested a portion of the dissertation some months before. Certain parts of a long document, such as the title, table of contents (including subheadings), and the literature review, are possible to draft early in a project and can give an editing manager two important pieces of information: the overall organization of the document and a preview of the quality of the writing. By requesting such a submission, the professor could have given the student feedback on the overall organization before the student had put everything on paper. The professor also could have established a writing standard for the student to meet in the remaining chapters.

Another consideration in keeping documents on schedule is to know your authors. Just as a baseball manager knows the players, their strengths and weaknesses, so too should you know the strengths and weaknesses of your authors. Some authors, for instance, are excellent at short documents, but have difficulty going the distance on a long report. Other authors actually prefer longer documents. For them, it is comforting to know that they will be working on the same project day in, day out, for an extended period.

Preference for a certain length is not the only aspect that distinguishes authors. Desire to collaborate is another. For instance, some authors (including this author) work much better as lone wolves. These authors prefer working in peaceful isolation until a draft is completed and an edit required. Others, such as my wife, prefer the influence and energy of others on a project. These authors are adept at compromising, dividing tasks, and providing support for one another. As an editor who has a say over which authors work on which projects, you can go a long way to having the authors meet their deadlines by matching the right authors with the right projects.

Providing Spoken and Written Feedback

The day after you arrive home from Munich, you come to the office early, groggy from the shift in time zones, but unable to sleep past five o'clock in the morning. Although Daulton, Leslie, and John are not yet in the office, you know that each is wondering about your response to his or her document. You question whether simply to hand them the documents or to spend the time, which you do not really have, to explain your comments. In the end, you decide to set up a formal meeting with Daulton because you have much to say to him. With Leslie, you will hand her the marked proposal in person, congratulate her on the fine job she did, and mention that you have just a few questions in the margins. With John, you will send him an e-mail with the words he wants to hear, "The article has been sent out."

Once I had an engineer come to my office to discuss a report that his supervisor had asked me to edit. As soon as the engineer walked through the door, I realized that this person was not prepared for the stern comments that I had written about his work. His face was red, his hands shook, and his neck was so tense that veins protruded. Rather than begin discussing the ways that this report could be strengthened (and in this case, there were many), I began discussing how difficult it was to communicate the work that he was trying to communicate. Following that, I mentioned how important this work was and how important it would be to communicate the work well. Then I discussed the aspects of the writing that he had done well and continued discussing those aspects until his neck relaxed. When he appeared ready to listen to criticism, I quietly discussed what aspects he needed to improve.

Is friction between editors and authors an inherent part of editing? To some degree, it is. Editing documents in business, engineering, and science is inherently challenging—the ideas are complex, the words to present those ideas are not exact, and often there is more than one successful way to express an idea. Because of the challenges, editing often involves argument—defending your positions—but that arguing does not have to descend to quarreling. Much depends on the editor's approach. As an editor, you can do much to reduce the friction between yourself and your authors.

First, you have to remember that editing is a two-way

communication. In some circumstances, such as a blind review of a journal article, you as a reviewer are constrained to give only written comments, and all communication filters through a journal editor. In most other types of edits, though, such as within a company, you have the opportunity to speak with the author. While writing down comments gives you the chance to mull over criticisms and make those criticisms more precise, speaking with the author allows you to find out the intentions of the author and, in so doing, to offer the changes that best serve those intentions.

Speaking with the author also allows you better control over the tone of the critique. Words can soften the slap that a cold page of editing changes often delivers, especially when that page requests the author to make major changes in the writing. In other words, when speaking to someone face to face, you have a better feel for when to soften the criticism. One supervisor, for instance, in editing the first report of a new hire had many comments that arose from making the content more precise. Although the paper looked as if it were bleeding, the supervisor was quite pleased with the new hire's writing effort. In returning the paper to him, she emphasized that point. As he looked over the many comments, he repeatedly questioned her, "But you think I did well?" "Very well," she said. In the end, the new hire accepted both the compliments on his writing and the changes he had to make.

In speaking with someone, you want to follow the

advice of Chapter 2 and begin with the positive. If your edit is solely negative, an author who may have invested much work into the document might see your criticism as an attack and then tune you out. Remember: Your goal as an editor is not to find every weakness in the document, but to provide an edit that will cause the author to produce the best possible document. For that reason, a strong edit acknowledges what the author has done well. As mentioned in Chapter 2, acknowledging the strengths of the writing does not translate to giving false praise or to delivering equal amounts of time for strengths as for weaknesses. It simply means providing a context for your criticisms.

Another advantage that speaking with the author gives you is that you have yet another way to emphasize the most important points of your critique and to gauge whether those points have sunk in. For instance, once you have given the author a general criticism, such as "many sentences were imprecise," then conversing with the author allows you to discern whether your chosen examples of imprecision were sufficient to convince the author.

Of course, some situations do not afford you the time or the occasion for a conference with the author. What should you do when you do not have time to speak with an author? If you have relatively few comments on a document and if you know that the author will be comfortable with those comments, then speaking with that author is probably unnecessary. However, if you have substantial comments or are working with an author whom you do not know well, the situation could cause problems. In such a case, attach a cover sheet with your edit that provides an overall assessment. In the cover sheet, try to maintain a professional, but conversational, tone and offer the author the opportunity to discuss your comments when you do have time.

As a final consideration, continually remind yourself that not all authors are alike. Just as each author is individual in his or her writing abilities, each author is also individual in his or her response to criticisms. An approach that inspires one author might put off another. Moreover, becoming an effective editor for each author will often involve uncomfortable moments, particularly on the first couple of edits. However, that discomfort will eventually fade once you and your author fall into stride — your author understanding what you expect, and you understanding what your author can deliver.

Chapter 6

Editing: The Big Picture

How upset [Max Planck] was whenever he inadvertently gave out the wrong information, whether in scientific publication or casual conversation, since despite all efforts, he knew that at least some untruth would persist

Lise Meitner

The way that a document is drafted and edited varies greatly not only from institution to institution, but also from document to document within the same institution. For short documents, the drafting is often done by a single writer who has expertise on the subject. After that writer drafts the document, the document proceeds through an editing chain, which may be in series or in parallel. Many institutions, for example, have a simple sign-off chain: author to first-level manager to second-level manager and so on. In such a series chain, the author usually makes all the changes at one level before the document proceeds to the next. Once all have signed the document, the document is published.

With larger documents, such as proposals, the drafting and the editing are usually more complicated. Rather than have a single writer for the document, many institutions rely on several writers who collaborate to produce the document. Moreover, the editing often includes more than a simple sign-off chain. Common in proposal editing, for instance, is to have a "red team" that plays devil's advocate to the arguments made in the proposal. Also common in proposal editing is to have someone pitch the arguments of the likely competition. This simulated competition helps determine what the house proposal should include to counter or mitigate those arguments.

What can you glean from examining the strategies used by different institutions and the duties of editors within those institutions? First, you should realize that no universal system of editing professional documents exists. Many editing strategies have arisen in business, engineering, and science, and these differ in several ways: the stages at which documents are edited, the order in which the editors are arranged, and the roles that the editors play.

Another point to recognize is that historical events, particularly mistakes, within an institution have probably influenced the institution's editing strategy as much as anything. For instance, after the space shuttle *Challenger* disaster, the sign-off process for the documents of NASA contractors changed dramatically. Months before the disaster, engineers at Morton-Thiokol had voiced concerns in memoranda about such a disaster. For the most part, these concerns were lost in the paperwork. After the disaster, changes in the sign-off process were made to ensure that such concerns, no matter at what level they were voiced, would be heard.

A third point that you can learn from observing the range of editing strategies in business, engineering, and science is that any evaluation of an editing strategy, with respect to its effectiveness and efficiency, should consider the institution and the document. In other words, a strategy that is appropriate for a classified weapons report at Lawrence Livermore National Laboratory may not be appropriate for an internal proposal at General Electric.

At What Writing Stages Should Editing Occur?

At one of the national laboratories, I worked with a manager who refused to edit anything but the final typeset manuscript. Although we passed outlines and drafts of major documents across his desk, he made no mark until the final sign-off copy came. Unfortunately for us, his edits went well beyond the comments of form that you would expect for a typeset version of a document. This manager presented us with voluminous edits of content and structural aspects of style that required major reworkings of the document. Although his editing comments would have strengthened the document had they come earlier, they occurred so late in the writing process, often a few days before the deadline, that we either could not incorporate them or would incorporate them at the expense of creating several typographical errors.

When challenged on this strategy of waiting until the last version before actually reading and making comments, his response was that his time was too valuable to spend on a draft that the author had not thoroughly considered. The way he saw it, what was the point of his editing questions that the author and the other editors would resolve before the document came across his desk in a final form?

While the manager certainly had a point that heavy editing during the early writing stages can be wasted effort, I contend that editing during the early stages is not an all-or-nothing task. For instance, in looking at a detailed outline, a manager can discern what information the author has included and in what order that information appears. From that relatively quick observation, the manager is in a good position to comment on the organization of the document. Likewise on a draft, while a busy manager may not have the time to read every page and certainly should not spend the time marking repeated errors in form, the manager should at least read the introduction and conclusions. These two sections allow the manager to comment on the scope of the document and the emphasis of results.

Granted, some drafts are submitted that are so poorly conceived that they should be returned immediately to the author. However, to group all drafts in that way is an oversimplification and a cause for frustration for those authors who have taken the document as far as they can take it and now need feedback. To deny such authors feedback at that point actually makes the overall editing process not only less effective, but less efficient.

Who Shall Edit First and Who Shall Edit Last?

Two main strategies exist at the company or laboratory level for editing a manuscript: a series strategy and
a parallel strategy. In a series strategy, shown in
Figure 6-1, the manuscript proceeds through editors along
a chain until all editors have signed off. In some series
strategies, all changes have to be made at each link of the
chain before the manuscript moves on to the next editor.
In other series strategies, each manager edits the same
document (or computer file) such that the edits of the preceding editors can be seen. The principal advantage of a
series strategy is quality control — the highest-level manager knows exactly what is sent out.

In a parallel strategy, shown in Figure 6-2, each editor
receives a copy of the manuscript from the author and
edits simultaneously. The comments come back to the
author, who then incorporates them into the original. The
principal advantage of a parallel strategy is speed — the
time for the edit is only as long as the time for the slowest
editor to complete the edit.

Note that many institutions use variations of these

| Draft | Editor 1 | Editor 2 | Editor 3 | Final |

Figure 6-1. Series editing strategy. Sometimes in this strategy, the author performs the requested changes between edits. In other situations, the author waits until all editors have marked the draft.

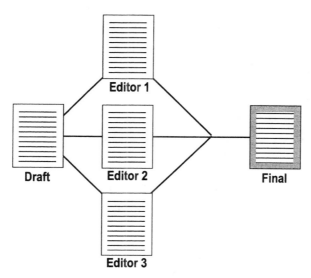

Figure 6-2. Parallel editing strategy.

paths. For instance, an institution might use a parallel strategy for editing drafts and a series sign-off for the document's final version. As with so many aspects of the writing or editing process, there is no magic formula that will work for all situations. The following subsections examine these two major strategies in more detail so that you can assess when to apply each strategy.

Series Strategy. In the 1990s, a state legislature created a new advisory committee requiring representation from several state agencies. Assigned to set up this committee, an engineer with the state's Department of Agriculture wrote a one-page letter requesting a representative from each agency. At the Department of Agriculture, such a letter had to be approved by a series of five managers, beginning with the engineer's immediate supervisor and ending with the secretary of agriculture. The sign-off procedure required that the letter not move to the next level until the engineer had made all requested changes. From the first three levels, the engineer received several comments regarding transitions, word choices, and punctuation. Nonetheless, for the first three levels, in passing from one level to the next, the number of comments declined such that the letter started to take shape.

At the fourth level, though, the engineer received a full page of comments addressing not only transitions, word choices, and punctuation, but rhythm and order of details within sentences. In fact, this manager had reworked every sentence. After making the requested changes, the engineer resubmitted the letter to this fourth-level manager, only to receive another full page of comments, some of which returned sentences to their original forms.

This story illustrates the difficulties with a series process. A series process ensures that the editor at the end of the series sees the document in its final form. Because an institution can dictate who has the final edit, the institution has much control on the final output of the document. While this strategy can be effective at controlling what goes out, the strategy can be inefficient when the latter editors request needless changes. For a series scheme to work well, the editors should understand their roles. Editors at the end should assume a more defensive posture as far as what to change. Certainly, these editors should insist on changing anything that would endanger or embarrass the institution. However, these editors should not quibble about the gray areas of style and form, especially when quibbling with these areas involves many changes.

Parallel Strategy. At one of the national laboratories, an annual report that was behind schedule required a final edit from three managers before going to the printer. Because the report was behind schedule, the managers agreed to edit the report simultaneously. The comments from all the managers came back quickly, the changes were incorporated by the report's author, and the report made it to the printer on time. However, after the report was published and distributed, one of the managers screamed bloody murder because another manager had changed the wording of a sentence such that, in the angry manager's opinion, the report now delivered a false impression. This angry manager was particularly upset that he had not had the opportunity to review the altered sentence.

This story illustrates the difficulties in trying to devise an effective parallel editing scheme. A parallel scheme can speed the editing process because all editors review the document simultaneously. This speed is an advantage with respect to efficiency: A document that would take weeks to move through a series sign-off chain can pass through a parallel chain in days. This potential for speed is also a disadvantage with respect to effectiveness when authors do not or cannot meet their responsibility of informing editors of major changes. If one editor requests a major change, then the author has the responsibility of informing the other editors of that change.

For a parallel strategy to work well, editors have to be sensitive to gray areas of style and form, and not place the author in the middle of a battle between two editors over such issues. Moreover, the editors and the author have to be clear about the process. For instance, if a major change occurs during the editing process, then all the editors should have the opportunity to review that change. However, if only minor changes occur, the author should be allowed to use his or her discretion as to whether to inform the editors. Otherwise, the parallel process loses its advantage of speed because if the author were to inform every editor of every comma that moves during the editing process, then the parallel process would go through several iterations and take even longer than the series process.

The main problem with this "major and minor" system for the parallel strategy lies in deciding which changes are major and which are minor. Criteria for such decisions have to be agreed upon before the editing process begins, and the author, if in doubt, should consult the editors.

What Role Should Each Editor Play?

A third variable in examining the overall editing strategies of institutions is the role that each editor plays. As has been discussed, three types of suggestions are made by editors: suggestions on the content, suggestions on the style, and suggestions on the form. At many institutions, managers have free reign with their edits — from content to style to form. At other institutions, editors are constrained to address only one or two of these aspects. For instance, at some institutions, when a legal department manager examines a document, the sole purpose is a content edit, and the perspective on that content edit is restricted to legal issues. Likewise, when an accounting manager edits the document, the sole purpose is a content edit, and the perspective on that content edit is accounting. Moreover, when a technical writer with the institution edits the document, the sole purpose is an edit for style and form.

So which of these two strategies (free reign or restricted reign) is stronger? The answer is not clear-cut. The first strategy is troublesome when the editors take hard-line positions about gray areas of style and form. For example, if one manager insists upon the spelling *focussing* and then another manager changes that spelling to *focusing*, what could ensue is a tug of war over a meaningless issue (both spellings are accepted). For the first strategy to work well, each editor should recognize what his or her expertise is and not be shy about editing on that turf. Likewise, each editor should recognize what areas of expertise the other members have and tread upon that turf with respect. Showing respect might mean raising questions about an issue rather than simply calling for changes.

With the second strategy, the boundaries are difficult to define. Although this book has tried to sort edits into the categories of content, style, and form, these categories overlap. For instance, the precision with which an idea is expressed is a matter of both content and style. Such overlaps pose a problem with adopting the second strategy. Another weakness of the second strategy is that the possibility of missing valuable edits is also high. For instance, a manager in accounting might have excellent advice about the design of an illustration, or a technical writer might recognize that a key detail has been omitted from a process description. In a strict adherence to this second strategy, those edits would be lost.

Not only do the categories of editing (content, style, and form) define an editor's role, but so does the depth at which the editor edits within each category. Some institutions say nothing about how much depth an editor should take on. Other institutions say a great deal. For instance, the Jet Propulsion Laboratory specifies eighteen items that an editor should consider when examining format [Van Buren and Buehler, 1980].

Even if your institution does not specify to what depth you should edit, you should establish a level for content, style, and form for which you assume responsibility. Granted, for each of these categories, you can exhaust yourself by going to the nth degree. For that reason, at some level, you have to say "enough." Where you draw that line depends on several variables: the time you have for editing; the personality of the author with whom you are working; the idiosyncracies of the other editors with whom you are working; and the purpose and importance of the document itself. As with so many issues of editing, these variables have to be balanced.

This chapter has examined editing from the institution's perspective. As was shown, no universal strategy exists for editing a document. Moreover, many variables, including past mistakes, influence the strategies of different institutions. What is important is that you understand your editing role in your institution's strategy. What is also important is that you understand the strategy's strengths and weaknesses. With that understanding, you are prepared to advocate a change in the strategy for a particular document if the strategy does not serve that document.

One Hundred Problems of Style

Style has no fixed laws; it is changed by the usage of the people, never the same for any length of time.

Seneca

The word "style" has multiple meanings in writing. When used as a noun, the word often refers to the choices of structure, language, and illustration that the author controls. However, when the word "style" is an adjective modifying the word "manual" or "guide," the meaning broadens to include aspects of format, grammar, punctuation, and usage that are either often executed incorrectly or not universally agreed upon. This appendix uses the word "style" in this second sense to discuss one hundred problems that often trip managers, scientists, and engineers when they attempt to edit.

In this appendix, one category of problems, indicated by a pencil (✎), follows the narrower definition of style — those aspects of structure, language, and illustration that vary from writer to writer. From this category, common problems are redundancies, pretentious words, and unanchored abstract nouns. In general, the problems from this category pertain to a lack of precision, clarity, or conciseness in the writing.

A second category of problems, indicated by 𝕵𝕱, addresses the format of the writing. When you create a document, you are faced with many formatting decisions, from choosing a typeface to selecting the amount of white space that precedes a heading. In making these decisions you want to choose a typeface and layout that are easy to read, that are in accord with the document's purpose, and that present the work in such a way that the most important details stand out. Given the wide selection of typefaces and layouts, you should consult an artist. Most artists have spent years studying different designs and can select a typeface and layout to meet your needs. In situations that do not allow you time to consult an artist, you will have to select the typeface and layout yourself. To help you with such decisions, the listings from this category present the format choices used at Sandia National Laboratories [1990].

A third category of problems, indicated by a bullet (●), presents common mistakes of grammar, punctuation, usage, and spelling. The severity of the mistake is indicated by the darkness of the bullet:

- ● unsettles many readers to the point of their losing confidence in the author or misreading the content
- ● either distracts many readers, or distracts only a few readers but affects the content
- ● distracts only a few readers and does not affect content

Severity depends on two variables: how many readers notice the error, and how much the error affects those readers. With an error such as confusing *affect* and *effect* (●), many readers are unsettled to the point of losing confidence in the author. For instance, the audience might question how much reading this author does. With an error such as confusing *compose* and *comprise* (●), many readers are distracted, but not unsettled. With an error such as confusing *enormity* and *enormousness* (also ●), not as many readers are distracted, but those distracted notice a change in the content. Finally, with an error such as using *due to* when *because of* is called for ( ), only a few readers are distracted and content is not affected.

My ranking of errors in this appendix is not universal because, as discussed in Chapter 3, not everyone responds to errors in the same way. An error such as a split infinitive, which is often ignored by professional editors, still sends a few mossbacks into convulsions. As Fowler [1965] states, some people "would sooner have their eyes gouged than split an infinitive." In assessing the amount of distraction, I have tried to side with the majority of language experts, many of whose opinions you can find in the works listed in the bibliography at the end of this appendix. Although this assessment is by no means universal, it does provide you a guide for deciding how much energy to devote to advocating a change.

Many of the errors from the third category of listings I have learned the hard way, by making the mistakes in my writing and then being chided after the publication came out. Generally, these misuses arose from what my eyes and ears assumed to be correct, but turned out to be otherwise. As mentioned earlier in this book, I grew up in southern Appalachia, an area of the country not renowned for its adherence to the accepted rules of English. Now, I am not using my roots to make excuses for past errors — those mistakes are my responsibility — but I do want to point out how easy it is to be influenced by the language we hear. For instance, how many times have you heard someone say *center around, irregardless, is comprised of,* or *very unique?* Although none of these phrases are proper English, all are widely used.

In addition to cataloguing the different problems of style, this appendix uses opposing arrows (↔) to identify problems upon which editors disagree. In some cases, such as when to use numerals (*1, 2, 3*) and when to write out numbers (*one, two, three*), the source for the disagreement is easy to identify: different format conventions. In other cases, such as whether to use *I* or *we*, the source for the disagreement is difficult to pinpoint. No matter what the source of disagreement is, you should not use this guide as an answer key to dictate which choice is right and which is wrong. The terms "right" and "wrong" do not apply in these controversial cases. Rather, you should use this guide as a reference from which you can decide the convention, or "style," that is appropriate for your situation — your audience, your purpose, your occasion.

a, an (●) Use *an* for indefinite singular nouns that begin with vowel sounds: an atom, an egret, an intern, an orangutan, an ultraviolet ray, an hour. Use *a* for indefinite nouns that begin with a consonant sound: a llama, a hysterectomy, a utility ("y" sound). Notice that as the pronunciation of a word changes over time, the article before it may change as well. As mentioned in Chapter 3, when the "h" in *historical* was silent, *an* preceded the word. When the "h" became pronounced, *a* preceded it. Notice also that a gray area exists with abbreviations such as *UV*. If your audience reads the abbreviation as "you vee," then use *a*. However, if your audience reads the abbreviation as "ultraviolet," then use *an*. If your audience could read the abbreviation either way, then choose one article (*a* or *an*) and remain consistent.

abbreviation (✎) Because abbreviations generally add complexity to the writing, you should avoid them. Many abbreviations call for adding periods to the writing. What is wrong with that? you ask. What is wrong is that periods are your most powerful pieces of punctuation. They are stop signs signaling the end of a complete thought. However, using periods for abbreviations dilutes their power to stop. For that reason, it is more fluid to write out the words *figure* and *versus* than to write the abbreviations *fig.* and *vs.* as so many journal formats prescribe.

In other cases, abbreviations call for using **all capital letters,** which makes the writing appear more complex. In some cases, where a complex term such as *magnetohy-*

drodynamics is used several times in a document, the abbreviation *MHD* saves the reader time. However, if the term is used only once or twice, then write it out. Certain abbreviations such as *AIDS* and *IBM* have become more familiar to audiences than the original terms: *acquired immunodeficiency syndrome* and *International Business Machines*. In such cases, you should rely on the abbreviation. Note, though, that in the case of *United States* or *U.S.*, readers expect you to write *United States* when a noun is called for ("in the United States"). When an adjective is called for, readers are accustomed to seeing *U.S.* ("the U.S. economy").

Finally, shy away from slang abbreviations, such as *btw* (by the way). Not only do these abbreviations add needless complexity, but they also erect a communication barrier to those who have not yet learned the slang.

-ability words (✎) A word ending in *ability* is a signal that you can tighten the sentence. Although a word such as *capability* is no big deal, pretentious constructions such as *expandability* and *manufacturability* are. Rewrite such sentences using *expansion* and *can manufacture*.

abstract nouns (✎) Abstract nouns are nouns that offer none of the five senses to the audience. Common abstract nouns in professional writing are *environment, factor,* and *nature*. When your writing contains too many abstract nouns, you risk losing your readers, who will have ceased seeing, hearing, smelling, tasting, or touching the details. What do you do if an abstract noun is a key word in the document? In such a case, you can give the abstract noun meaning by grounding it with an example the first time it appears.

active voice, passive voice (✎) In general, the active voice (the subject performs the action) is a more natural way to communicate, because it is crisper and more efficient than the passive voice. However, for those occasions in which the subject of your writing is acted upon, the passive voice is more natural. Although you should opt for the natural voice, avoid having strings of passive constructions in your writing. Such strings deflate the energy of the writing. (Also see **first person**.)

adverse, averse (◐) The word *adverse* means unfavorable, and the word *averse* means in opposition to: "Because of the adverse preliminary results, we were averse to continuing the funding."

affect, effect (●) *Affect* is almost always a verb with the meaning to influence. *Effect*, on the other hand, is usually a noun and means a result ("greenhouse effect"). A cause for confusion is that *effect* can also be used as a verb meaning to bring about: "She effected the change of orders." Adding even more confusion to the situation is that in the field of psychology, *affect* is used as a noun with the meaning of "emotional response."

Should one of your authors have a problem differentiating between these two words, then you should recommend that he or she use *affect* solely as a verb meaning to influence and use *effect* solely as a noun meaning a result.

alignment (𝕁) Most formats in professional writing use an alignment in which the text is either aligned on both the right and left margins or aligned on the left, but left ragged on the right. If both your printer and word processing program have proportional spacing, it makes little difference which of these two alignments you choose. Some people prefer the clean and formal look of text aligned on both sides; others prefer the natural look of text left ragged on the right. If either your printer or your word processing program does not have proportional spacing, then you should choose a ragged right margin. Otherwise, your text will have rivers of white space.

all capital letters (𝕁) Because text displayed in all capital letters is difficult to read, avoid using all capitals, especially in large blocks such as on presentation overheads. When people read words, they do not read every single letter; rather, to recognize the shapes of many words and syllables, they rely on the ascenders (*b, d, f, h, k, l, t*) and the descenders (*g, j, p, q, y*). When you use all capital letters, readers lose that recognition and read more slowly. One instance in which it is acceptable to use all capitals is in short titles or headings in which no alternative such as boldface, larger lettering, or placement exists to make the title or heading stand apart. Another instance is in the call-out of an illustration in which lowercase lettering would be too small to read.

alot (●) There is no such word as *alot*. There is, however, the noun phrase *a lot*. Because many consider this phrase to be informal, it is risky to use in professional documents.

alright (●) There is no such word as *alright*. What should be written in such cases is the phrase *all right*.

alternate, alternative, option ( ) Strictly speaking, the noun *option* refers to a choice among three or more things: "To treat this disease, we have three options." Likewise, the noun *alternative* refers to a choice between two things: "To measure temperature, we have two alternatives." Finally, the noun *alternate* refers not to a choice, but to a substitute: "He is the alternate for the committee." With regard to the adjective *alternate*, it refers to something that occurs in turns, one after the other: "The zebra's coat is marked by alternate stripes of black and white." These distinctions are fading. For instance, almost all publications accept the phrases "several alternatives" and "alternate route."

always, never (✎) *Always* and *never* are frightening words because they challenge readers to think of exceptions. If an exception exists and your readers find it, your authority will be undercut. Go in fear of absolutes.

amount, number (●) In general, use *amount* for items that cannot be counted and *number* for items that can. For that reason, write "a huge amount of water," "a paltry amount of grain," and "a significant amount of fish left on the plate." Likewise, write "a number of cells," "a number of errors," and "a number of fish in the stream." Note that *amount* is used with sums of money, as in "a large amount of money."

and/or (see **slash**)

anxious, eager (⬤) In formal writing, the word *anxious* means awaiting something with apprehension, while *eager* means awaiting something with enthusiasm. Therefore, if an author were to write, "I anxiously await your reply," it would suggest that he or she is expecting the worst. If the author awaits with positive expectations, he or she should write, "I eagerly await your reply."

approximately (✎) The word *approximately* is appropriate when used to modify a measurement's accuracy to within a fraction, but inappropriate when applied to a situation such as "approximately twelve people." Does the author mean 11.75 or 12.25 people? In such cases, have the author use the simple word *about*.

as, because (✎) The word *as* causes ambiguity because it has several meanings, including "when" and "because." This ambiguity can confuse readers: "As the antigens entered the bloodstream, the lymphocytes appeared." Although the author intended the sentence to mean that the lymphocytes appeared because the antigens entered the bloodstream, readers could easily misinterpret the sentence to mean that the lymphocytes happened to appear when the antigens entered. Because of the inherent ambiguity, have your authors choose the word *because* rather than *as* when they want the meaning "because." (Also see **as, like**.)

as, like (⬤) In formal writing, the word *like* is strictly a preposition and introduces prepositional phrases: "Like Earth, the planet Mars has an elliptical orbit." The word *as* is a conjunction and introduces clauses: "The airfield looks as it did in 1937 when the Hindenburg dirigible exploded." Although this distinction, once strong, is fading, many publications such as the *Wall Street Journal* still hold to the rule.

because of, due to ( ) The phrase *due to* modifies a noun: "The failure was due to the low temperature." The phrase *because of* is for modifying verbs: "The steel failed because of the low temperature." If the phrase follows any verb other than the verb *to be*, use *because of*. If the phrase introduces the sentence, use *because of*. If in doubt, use *because of*.

bi- (●) The prefix *bi-* means twice. Confusion arises over whether the prefix means that you multiply by two or divide by two. For the most part, *bi-* means that you multiply by two. For instance, *biennial* means once every two years, and *bimonthly* means once every two months. An exception, though, is *biannual*, which means semiannual, or twice a year.

bibliography (𝔍) A bibliography is an alphabetical listing of sources that were consulted in the writing of a document. Typically, a bibliography does not have its **reference citations** correspond to specific **reference listings** within the text of the document. For that reason, the connection between these sources and the assertions in the text is often not apparent. While some respected publications use this informal referencing system for articles, you can be sure that the home offices of those publications retain a copy of each article in which specific reference listings support each assertion. As for the form of the reference citations in the bibliography, those vary considerably.

capital letters in proper nouns (✎) Capitalize the first letter of proper nouns: Avogadro's number, Department of Energy, Bragg angle. Because capital letters add a complexity to the writing, avoid unnecessary capitalizing of terms such as "bremsstrahlung," "x-ray," and "production phase." Note that the capitalizations of some terms fall in a gray area. For instance, do you write the "Space Shuttle Discovery" or the "space shuttle *Discovery*"? Both forms appear in the literature. In such cases, choose one form and remain consistent.

capital letters in titles and headings (𝕁𝕗) Most artists choose initial capital letters, as opposed to all capital letters, for titles and headings. One common convention for initial capitals is to capitalize the first letter of the first and last words — no matter what the words. Then, you capitalize the first letter of every included word except for articles, coordinating conjunctions, and prepositions that have fewer than five letters. Examples of words not capitalized are *a, an, and, but, for, in, into, nor, on, or, the, to, with,* and *yet.* Note that you would capitalize the short word *Is* because it is a verb.

center around (●) The phrase *center around* makes no physical sense. You should use either *center on* or *revolve around.*

clichés (✎) Clichés are descriptive phrases that have become trite. Common examples are *come up to speed, sticks* *out like a sore thumb,* and *greatest thing since sliced bread.* If a descriptive phrase sounds cute, avoid it.

colon (●) When a colon introduces a list, definition, example, or equation, what appears on the left side of the colon should stand alone as a separate sentence:

> We studied five types of marsupials: opossums, bandicoots, koalas, wombats, and kangaroos.

Colons should not, though, break continuing statements.

Mistake:	The five types of marsupials studied were: opossums, bandicoots, koalas, wombats, and kangaroos.
Correction:	The five types of marsupials studied were opossums, bandicoots, koalas, wombats, and kangaroos.

Note that when a sentence follows a colon, you capitalize the first letter of that sentence.

comma, after an introductory phrase or clause (●) Commas are used to separate introductory phrases and clauses from the main part of the sentence:

> As light hydrocarbons evaporate, the oil vapor pressure falls.

When writers omit this comma, confusion often results. If in doubt, insist on using this comma, especially after *however* (when it's used as an adverb), clauses, and gerunds.

Mistake:	When feeding sharks sometimes mistake undesired items such as metal for food.
Correction:	When feeding, sharks sometimes mistake undesired items such as metal for food.

commas, parenthetical (●) Commas are used to separate parenthetical items in a sentence:

> The antivenin from that cobra's venom, which we extracted
> only last week, has become contaminated.

When the inserted item serves to define what comes before, no parenthetical commas are used:

> The antivenin that counteracts this cobra's bite was created
> only last week. *(the* that *clause defines which antivenin)*

A common mistake is to place a single parenthetical
comma between the subject and verb:

> Mistake: A huge earthquake of magnitude greater than
>   8.0, occurs each year somewhere in the world.
>
> Correction: A huge earthquake of magnitude greater than
>   8.0 occurs each year somewhere in the world.

commas, in a series (⬤↔) Life once was simpler. According
to William Strunk [1918], in a series of three or more items,
you should place a comma after each item except for the
last. Following this advice, you would write "oxygen, carbon, and hydrogen." Literary writers and journalists,
though, often drop the last comma in this series: "oxygen, carbon and hydrogen." This dropping of the series
comma poses a problem in professional documents,
which often have complicated lists: "lakes, rivers, streams
and man-made sources such as impoundments, drainage ditches and reservoirs." Without commas after
"streams" and "drainage ditches," the reader is not sure
how to group items in this list. Those favoring the
dropped-comma convention say that where ambiguities
arise, then insert the final comma. However, in professional writing, the possibility of ambiguity arises often,
and when the comma is missed, especially in instructions

and proposals, the consequences can be costly. Strunk's way is simpler—I recommend a return to the so-called series comma for professional writing.

Note that in a series of just two items, you use no comma unless the list can be misread. For that reason, write "bears and wolves." In situations where misreading can occur, include the comma: "bears with cubs, and wolves with pups."

comma splice (see **run-on sentence**)

compare to, compare with ( ) When using criteria to compare things that belong to the same class, use *compare with*: "In his study, Barnhart compared drug treatments with radiation treatments." When making an analogy to something of a different class, use *compare to*: "Freud compared the relationship of the ego and the id to a horse and its rider."

compose, comprise (●) The word *comprise* literally means to include. Most conservative sources such as Cook [1985] hold to that literal definition. For that reason, conservative sources insist on the whole comprising the parts, not the reverse. Moreover, conservative sources shun the phrase *is comprised of* because it makes no sense.

conjunctions to begin sentences (✎↔) Coordinating conjunctions, such as *and* and *but*, are powerful words that connect words, phrases, and clauses. Is it proper to begin sentences with conjunctions? Although some formal scientific journals frown on this usage, many respected publications, including the *New York Times,* allow it. Should you decide to live on the wilder side and begin a sentence with an *and* or *but,* do not place a comma after the conjunction. If you want the pause that comma provides, begin the sentence with *in addition* or *however* followed by the comma.

continual, continuous (⬤) The word *continual* means repeatedly: "For two weeks, the sperm whales continually dived to great depths in search of food." The word *continuous* means without interruption: "The spectrum of light is continuous." Given this distinction, the commonly used phrase "make continuous improvements" is an exaggeration unless the parties making the improvements do not sleep or break for meals.

contractions ( ) The more formal the professional document is, the less accepted are common contractions such as *can't, don't,* and *it's.* Not accepted are seldom-used contractions such as *would've* or *could've.*

criterion, criteria (⬤) *Criterion* is the singular form, and *criteria* is the plural form. Note that the Greek origin of this word accounts the unusual plural form. The same plural form occurs with *phenomenon (phenomena).*

dashes (⬤) Dashes come in several varieties. The em-dash (—), which is the length of an *m,* sets off parenthetical remarks that cannot be set off by commas:

> The unique feature of the design is a continuous manifold, which follows a unidirectional — as opposed to serpentine — flow for the working fluid.

Be careful with the em-dash. Too many em-dashes will break the continuity of your writing.

The en-dash (–), which is the length on an *n*, shows ranges ("10–20 amps") and separates words within compounds made up of like items ("electron–hole pair" or "Mordell–Weil Theorem").

A third type of dash, the **hyphen** (-), separates elements of compound terms such as "half-life," "three-fourths," and "cross-sectional."

data as a singular (⟷ **)** The word *data* is a plural form of *datum*, a Latin word. Because *datum* is seldom used as the singular form, many sources consider *data* acceptable as either singular or plural. Some conservatives, though, refuse to accept this word as singular. If you need a singular form and do not want to distract your conservative audience, spend an extra word and write *data point*.

different from, different than (● **)** Use the phrase *different from* and you will not be wrong: "This design is much different from the others." As Bernstein [1965] points out, odd occasions arise in which using *different from* causes cumbersome constructions, such as "different from that which." In these odd cases, substituting "different than" is acceptable. Otherwise, it is not.

effect (see **affect, effect**)

enormity, enormousness (●) Everyone agrees that *enormousness* means "a huge size." Those with a liberal view of language accept that *enormity* also has this definition. In the eyes of conservatives, though, *enormity* has only one meaning: "a monstrous or horrible act." For that reason, in the eyes of conservatives, the engineer who wrote the phrase "the enormity of our solar tower" degraded his own work.

ensure, insure (●) In British English, *ensure* means "to make sure or certain," and *insure* means "to guarantee with insurance against risk or loss of life." American English, on the other hand, allows *insure* to have both meanings. If your audience includes those educated in the United Kingdom, then you should distinguish as well.

equations (✍) Several formats exist for incorporating equations. This appendix presents one:

Center and set apart equations from the text with white space. Using arabic numerals, number those equations that are referred to in the text. An example is

$$S = 2\pi\mu r. \tag{1}$$

When referring to equations, call them by their names: equation 1, equation 2, and so on. Also, when incorporating an equation, treat it as part of the sentence that introduces the equation: "The voltage V is given by

$$V = I R, \tag{2}$$

where I is the current and R is the resistance."

facilitate (✍) The word *facilitate* is a bureaucrat's word. Opt for simpler wording such as *cause* or *bring about*.

farther, further (●) Conservative sources distinguish between *farther* and *further*, advocating that *farther* be used for distance and that *further* be used for all other variables: time, intensity, and so on. However, some conservative sources, including Bernstein [1965], admit that *further* will eventually become accepted for all uses.

fewer, less (⬤) In general, use *fewer* for items that can be counted and *less* for items that cannot. For that reason, write "fewer cells," "fewer errors," and "fewer fish in the stream." Likewise, write "less water," "less air," and "less foliage." Note that you usually treat money and time as continuous quantities: "less than 1 million dollars" and "less than 100 years ago."

figures, incorporating into documents (𝓕) Figures include photographs, drawings, diagrams, and graphs. In formal writing, the convention is that each figure appears below the end of the paragraph that introduces that figure. If not enough space is available below the end of the paragraph, then the text continues for the rest of that page, and the illustration appears at the top of the next page. When placing an illustration into a document, leave more space between the illustration and the text than you leave between the illustration and its caption.

Captions for figures appear below the figure, as shown in Figure A-1. A figure caption contains a phrase that identifies the figure. In some formats, the caption also contains a sentence or two that explains important details in the figure. When referring to figures, call them by their names. A common convention is Figure 1, Figure 2, Figure A-1, Figure B-1, and so forth. In this convention, Figure A-1 appears in Appendix A, and Figure B-1 appears in an Appendix B.

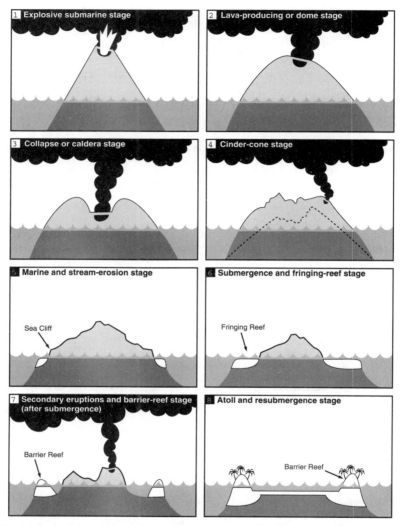

Figure A-1. Eight stages of a Hawaiian volcano [Bullard, 1976]. The first four stages constitute the building stages, and the remaining four constitute the declining stages.

first person (✎↔) First person refers to the use of *I* or *we*. One hundred years ago, first person occurred often in professional writing. For some reason, its use fell out of favor, but in the last fifteen years its use has reemerged. Occasional use of the first person can help break up strings of unwanted passive voice. As long as the emphasis remains on the subject of the writing, there is nothing inherently wrong with using the first person. Moreover, you can reduce the emphasis on a first-person pronoun by having the sentence begin with a prepositional or infinitive phrase. Even with those precautions, you should understand that some managers to their deaths will forbid its use in formal professional writing.

foreign words (✎↔) When incorporating foreign expressions into English, you should place those words in italics. Note, though, that once an expression has been used long enough, the italics are often dropped, such as with "in vitro," "in situ," and "cliché." Some expressions appear to be moving from italics to normal type—for instance, "*et al.*" is written in some journals, but "et al." is written in others. In such cases, choose what is in line with your document's format and the audience's expectations.

Note that many foreign expressions such as "e.g." add unnecessary complexity to the writing (see **abbreviations**).

fragments (●) While sentence fragments are accepted in informal writing such as advertisements, they are not accepted in formal writing. One exception does exist and has the following form: "The higher the temperature, the higher the pressure." In this exception, the verb *is* is understood to follow both "temperature" and "pressure."

good, well (⬤) By definition, adjectives such as *good* or *efficient* modify nouns and pronouns. Also, by definition, adverbs such as *well* or *efficiently* modify verbs, adjectives, and other adverbs (granted, *well* is sometimes an adjective, but with a different meaning). Given these definitions, you should not use an adjective such as "good" or "efficient" to modify a verb's action:

| Incorrect: | The design worked so good the first time that we didn't bother making changes. |
| Correct: | The design worked so well the first time that we didn't bother making changes. |

Likewise, do not use the comparative form of an adjective, such as *quicker*, to do a job that a comparative adverb, such as *more quickly*, should do:

| Incorrect: | This computer chip processes data much quicker than the older chips do. |
| Correct: | This computer chip processes data much more quickly than the older chips do. |

he or she (✎↔) Some languages have a singular pronoun to refer to an unspecified person regardless of gender. English, unfortunately, does not. For that reason, you should be sensitive to the way that you refer to an unspecified person. Just using *he* has become unacceptable in many contexts. So what should you do? The best solution is to use the plural form (*they*), which is gender neutral, to circumvent the problem. In cases where the plural is not an option, use *he or she*, which is an alphabetical listing of our singular pronouns. Note that relying strictly on alphabetical order causes a problem with the adjective forms (*her or his*) when *he or she* is in the same discussion. In such cases, use *his or her* to remain consistent in the reference. Avoid the ugly *he/she* and the even uglier *s/he*. The physical shapes of these words have undesirable connotations.

headings (ℐ) Several formats exist for headings, subheadings, and sub-subheadings, one of which is shown in Figure A-2. In this format, the typography and placement of the headings distinguish their hierarchy. This system changes somewhat with the document's length. In short reports, the major heading is the report's title, while in longer reports, the major headings serve as the names of the sections—for example, "Introduction" or "Conclusion." In these longer reports, the major headings follow one another in a continuous fashion, unless the reports are very long, in which case the major headings begin on new pages.

Many authors like to use numbers to show the hierarchy of headings (1.0, 1.0.1, 1.0.1.1). While such a system might serve a huge instruction manual that includes many internal references to other sections, this system is needlessly complex for most professional documents and does not visually reveal the hierarchy of headings as well as a system based on placement and typography does.

Another consideration for headings occurs in formatting electronic files. In such cases, using a defined format such as Heading 1, Heading 2, and Heading 3 has many advantages. By simply redefining the particular heading format, you can change the format for all the headings of that level in the document. In long documents, this ability to make global changes can save much time.

>
>
>
Major Heading
>
>

    For major headings, skip three carriage returns from the top margin (or previous section) and place the heading. Use 14 or 18 points, initial capitals, and boldface. For minor reports, the major heading serves as the report's title.
>
>

First Subheading
>

    Subheadings are 12 or 14 points, flush left, and boldfaced. For all subheadings, skip two lines before and one line afterwards. Use initial capitals for all subheadings. Note that a sans serif font is acceptable for headings and subheadings.
>

    First Sub-Subheading. Sub-Subheadings are placed in 12 point type, indented, boldfaced, and followed by a period. Skip one line before a sub-subheading. Begin the sub-subheading's text after the period. Use initial capitals for sub-subheadings.
>

    Second Sub-Subheading. If you have one sub-subheading, you must have a second. Otherwise, the first sub-subheading has nothing to be parallel with.
>
>

Second Subheading
>

    If you have one subheading, you must have a second. Otherwise, the first subheading has nothing to be parallel with.
>
>

page #

Figure A-2. Hierarchy for headings, subheadings, and sub-subheadings. Note that the box surrounding these headings represents the margin borders (not the page borders). Also note that, for illustration purposes, the type sizes shown in this figure have been reduced. Finally, note that in most documents the sections and subsections will be substantially longer.

hopefully, to mean "it is hoped that" ( ) Just as **_regretfully_** means "in a manner full of regret," _hopefully_ means "in a manner full of hope":

Correct: We looked hopefully to the courts for a ruling on the contract dispute.

In formal writing, using _hopefully_ to mean "it is hoped that" unsettles conservative readers:

Mistake: Hopefully, the antibodies will destroy the cancer cells.

Correction: It is hoped that the antibodies will destroy the cancer cells.

While English has _hopefully_ to be analogous with _regretfully_, English does not have a word that is analogous with _regrettably_, which means "it is regretted that." For that reason, when you want to write "it is hoped that," you should write "it is hoped that."

however, beginning sentences with ( ) Usually, _however_ appears as an adverb (like _moreover_ or _therefore_). Used in this way, _however_ has the meaning "on the other hand." Is it proper to begin a sentence with the adverb _however_? Yes. Although it is often more graceful to place _however_ later in the sentence ("There were, however, three possible solutions"), beginning a sentence with _however_ is standard ("However, three possible solutions existed"). Note that when _however_ is used in this way, a comma follows it.

hyphen ( ) In deciding when to place a hyphen between compound words, consult your dictionary or _The Chicago Manual of Style_ [1993]. If the answer is still unclear, then check what is done in well-edited publications such as the _Wall Street Journal_ and _Scientific American_. If still unsure, lean toward inserting a hyphen if the term is an adjective ("cross-sectional flow") and not inserting a hyphen if the term is a noun ("cross sections").

I, me (●) Use *I* for subjects (also see **first person**), and use *me* for direct objects, indirect objects, and objects of prepositions. For that reason, write *between you and me*, not *between you and I*. A common error in which *me* is used instead of *I* occurs with clauses in which the verbs are understood:

Mistake: She does parallel tasks much more efficiently than me. *("me" is incorrect)*

Correction: She does parallel tasks much more efficiently than I. *(an understood verb, "do," follows "I")*

if, whether ( ) Opt for *whether* when indicating possibilities: "We must decide whether to use liquid sodium or molten salt." Opt for *if* when indicating condition: "We will use liquid sodium if we can be sure that it is safe."

impact, to mean "effect" ( ) Comets have impacts with planets, speeding cars have impacts with trees, but greenhouse gases have "effects" on global warming. At least, that is the feeling of many readers who believe that using *impact* for anything other than a physical collision is imprecise and overstated. Restricting the use of *impact* to physical collisions is not easy, though, because *impact* has lodged itself into several phrases such as "environmental impact statement" without much room for revision.

impact, used as a verb (●) More disconcerting to many readers than using *impact* as a noun to mean "effect" is using *impact* as a verb to mean "affect." This latter use you should simply avoid.

implement, as a verb (✎) The verb *implement* is a pet verb of bureaucrats. Consider substituting *put into effect* or *carry out*. These verb phrases are old and simple. They are the verb phrases that Winston Churchill would have used.

indents of paragraphs (¶↔) Although some formats call for no indents of paragraphs, most do, particularly those designed by professional artists. The World Wide Web is influencing this choice because some browsers do not recognize paragraph indents. Although most artists prefer to indent each paragraph, they often choose not to indent the first paragraph of a report or chapter.

interface, to mean "the meeting of people" (◐) The word *interface* means the interstitial boundary between two planes, phases, or systems ("a molecular interface," "an oil–water interface," or "a computer interface"). Unsettling is the use of *interface* involving the meeting of people. Given the closeness implied by the definition, the idea of professional people interfacing is, well, unprofessional.

irregardless (◐) The construction *irregardless* is not standard English. Use *regardless*.

its, it's (●) The word *its* is the possessive form of the pronoun *it* and means "of it." The word *it's* is a contraction and means "it is." A few hundred years ago, someone decided on these meanings. Accept them; learn them; write them.

-ize (✎) Verbs with the suffix *-ize* are often pretentious. Although some verbs such as *optimize* are acceptable, other verbs such as *prioritize* and *utilize* are haughty. Opt instead for short, old words such as *rank* and *use*. Nouns with the suffix *-ization* are also often pretentious. You should challenge *-ization* nouns and search for simpler substitutes. For example, replace *utilization* with *use*. In cases where you have monstrosities such as *prioritization*, you should rewrite the entire sentence in forthright English. As with *-ization* nouns and *–ize* verbs, *-ized* adjectives are often pretentious. You should challenge *-ized* adjectives and search for simpler substitutes. For example, replace *discretized* with *discrete* and *individualized* with *individual*.

lead, led (●) The present tense of the verb *to lead* is *lead*, and the past tense is *led*:

> Present tense: Strong managers lead by example.
> Past tense: Who led last month's meeting?

Although this rule is straightforward, many people mistakenly write *lead* for the past tense form. Confusing the issue for these wayward writers is the noun *lead* (Pb), which sounds like the past tense verb *led*, but is spelled like the verb's present tense *lead*.

lie, lay (●) *Lie* means to recline or rest on a surface: "The patient had such a severe rash that he could not *lie* still for more than a few seconds." *Lay* means to place or set down: "Lay the drugged calf carefully on its side." Confusion arises because the past tense of *lie* is *lay*: "Yesterday, the patient lay on his side." Note that the past tense of *lay* is *laid*: "Last night he laid the form on my chair."

lists (✎) In professional writing, lists are often complex. The best way to avoid ambiguity in the grouping of items in a list is to separate each item with a piece of punctuation (see **commas in a series** and **semicolon**). You can also use numbers to help separate the items. For some odd reason, perhaps a quirk in current software, people have begun using two pieces of punctuation such as *(1.)* to follow these numbers. One piece of punctuation suffices (remember the punishment given to Moses for striking the rock twice). I prefer the parenthesis and reserve the period for what it does best, ending sentences.

Vertical lists, in which you break out of the paragraph and list items vertically, are overused in professional writing. While such lists are appropriate for presenting tasks in a set of instructions, too many vertical lists will needlessly slow the reading of articles and reports. Reserve vertical formatting for those important lists that readers will search for on subsequent readings.

medium, media (●) *Medium* is the singular form, and *media* is the plural form. Note that the Latin origin of this word accounts for the unusual plural form. The same plural form occurs with *stratum (strata)*.

misplaced modifier (●) Have modifiers point to the words that they modify. Failure to follow this rule causes ambiguities. In the following example, the misplaced modifier is shown in italics.

Mistake: *Shooting at speeds of 100 mph*, the engineers tested the solar mirrors for hailstone damage.

Who or what was "shooting at 100 mph"?

Correction: To test for mirror damage, the engineers fired hail-
                stones at 100 mph onto the solar mirrors.

misspellings (●) Misspellings are different from simple
typos. In this book, a misspelling is defined as an incorrect spelling that a spell-checker would catch (writing
undoubtably as opposed to *undoubtedly*), while a **typo** is an
incorrect spelling that a spell-checker would miss (typing *ball* rather than *balk*). Misspellings often offend the
audience more than typos because misspellings suggest
that the author did not take the time to run a simple spell-
check. In some situations, such as posters or web pages,
performing spell-checks is difficult. Unfortunately, you
are held to the same standards. The words given below
are commonly misspelled in professional writing (the letters often missing or incorrect are in boldface):

accom**m**odate	man**eu**ver
acknowled**gm**ent	mill**e**n**n**ium
bureaucratic	occ**u**rred
calend**a**r	**pe**rform
depend**e**nt	rec**ei**ve
embarrassment	refe**rr**ed
ind**i**spensable	sep**a**rate
maintenance	substitute

more than, over ( ) To avoid tripping your readers, reserve the word *over* for physical position ("clouds passed
over the solar collector") and for range ("over the past 35
years"). When you are referring to one quantity exceed-
ing another, use *more than* or *greater than*: "The top of the
Tower of Pisa leans more than 5 meters off center."

more important, more importantly ( ) A common mistake is
to place *more importantly* at the beginning of a sentence to

indicate the meaning "what is more important." The correct choice in this case is *more important*:

More important, the cancer spread to the liver.

The adverbial phrase "more importantly" means something different: "in a more important manner":

In the assessment, the leak was viewed more importantly than it should have been.

nauseated, nauseous (⬤) The word *nauseated* means to feel sick to one's stomach, while the word *nauseous* means causing one to become sick. For that reason, you should write, "The fumes caused us to become nauseated." Here, the fumes are nauseous, but those who breathe the fumes become nauseated.

number (see **amount, number**)

numerals, when to write out (𝕵↔) Numerals are actual figures: 0, –1, 2.76, 3000. Because numerals add complexity to the writing, you should use numerals only when necessary. Several conventions exist for when to write out numbers. One is to write out numbers less than ten. Another, which I prefer, is to write out numbers that can be expressed in one or two words.

one	two thousand
thirteen	seventy-six

There are several exceptions for when to write out numbers, and these exceptions are universal. Some of these exceptions, such as illustration numbers (Figure 2), have arisen from format conventions. Other exceptions, such as negative numbers (–1) and decimals (0.3), have arisen from arithmetic conventions. Still other important exceptions have arisen for convenience and clarity:

specific measurements	12 meters/second
percentages	15 percent
consistency within paragraph	123, 44, and 9.
monetary figures	$3,450
large numbers	46 million, $3 million

Another exception in English is that one avoids beginning a sentence with a numeral. An improper beginning then would be

64.1 milligrams of copper corroded during the tests.

If a numeral is called for, you should restructure the sentence so that the numeral does not appear first:

During the tests, 64.1 milligrams of copper corroded.

only (✎) The word *only* is difficult to use correctly because it is an adjective sometimes and an adverb on other occasions. For that reason, its position in a sentence determines the meaning of the sentence:

Only Wallace checked the patient's wound.
Wallace only checked the patient's wound.
Wallace checked only the patient's wound.
Wallace checked the only patient's wound.
Wallace checked the patient's only wound.

In this example, there are five different positions of the word *only* and five different meanings for the sentence. Check the position of *only* to make sure that it modifies what you want it to modify.

panacea for (●) *Panacea* means a cure-all. Many people mistakenly misuse this word by saying a "panacea for" a class of problems. In such situations, *panacea* is inappropriate. What the writers should use is *cure*.

parallelism, faulty (●) In a list, present the items in a parallel fashion. In other words, if your first slice of pie is apple, then readers expect the remaining slices to be apple. In the following example, the nonparallel item appears in italics:

Mistake: The process involves three main steps: cooling, chopping, and *pulverization*.

Correction: The process involves three main steps: cooling, chopping, and pulverizing.

Parallelism is often lost in constructions involving *either...or, neither...nor,* and *not only...but also.* Such constructions require that what appears on the left side of the conjunction be parallel with what appears on the right.

Mistake: Our goal is either to predict or *measure* the speed.

Correction: Our goal is either to predict or to measure the speed.

penultimate (●) Often misused, *penultimate* is an adjective meaning next to the last. It is not a fancier way to express the meaning "ultimate."

phenomenon, phenomena (see **criterion, criteria**)

plethora, to mean simply "large number" (●) Often misused, *plethora* is a noun meaning an excess or overabundance. Many people do not realize the negative connotation associated with this abundance and mistakenly use *plethora* to indicate simply a large amount.

plurals of abbreviations and numerals (𝔍↔) While plurals for words are readily found in the dictionary, plurals of abbreviations and numerals fall into a gray zone, appearing with an apostrophe in some publications and without an apostrophe in other publications. I prefer forming these plurals without apostrophes so that no confusion exists with the singular **possessive** forms. For that reason, I write *CPUs* for the plural of *CPU* and *1990s* for the years between 1990 and 1999.

possessives (●) For most singular nouns, you form the possessive by adding *'s*: "a person's fingerprints," "someone else's decision," and "your boss's authority." Exceptions include a handful of people and places in which the possessive form does not add an *s* sound to the pronunciation (for instance, "Moses' Law," "Mount St. Helens' eruption," and "Archimedes' principle"). For most plural nouns, you form the possessive by adding an apostrophe: "the wolves' tracks in the snow." Exceptions include irregular plurals ("the children's flu shots").

principal, principle **(●)** The word *principal* can be either a noun or an adjective. As an adjective, *principal* means main or most important. The word *principle* appears only as a noun and means a law, as in "Archimedes' principle."

quotation marks, misplacement of (●) In the United States, periods and commas appear inside of end quotation marks. In Great Britain, however, periods and commas appear inside only if they belong to the quoted material. Otherwise, these pieces of punctuation appear outside. For those publishing in the United States, the rule is simple. Learn it and follow it.

> U.S. Mistake: Seaborg claimed that the reactor "will produce the power of Hoover Dam, from a cold start, in a matter of minutes".

U.S. Correction: Seaborg claimed that the reactor "will produce the power of Hoover Dam, from a cold start, in a matter of minutes."

reading level (✎) Reading level, sometimes called the fog index [Gunning, 1952], is a measure of the complexity of the sentences and words in a piece of writing. For instance, a tenth grader could manage the sentence lengths and word lengths in a document with a reading level of 10. Just because a document has a level of 10 does not mean that a tenth grader could understand the content, though. Likewise, a document with a reading level of 20 may not necessarily present sophisticated ideas. All it means is that whatever ideas there are (from talk show babble to quantum electrodynamics), the document presents those ideas in a complex fashion. Another way to think about the reading level is with respect to the amount of concentration required of a reader just to sort the relationships of words in sentences.

Because professional writing contains challenging ideas, you want the reading level to be low so that your reader can focus on what you have to say and not on how you say it. A reasonable level would be between 9 and 12. The *New York Times* and the *Wall Street Journal* have reading levels of 11. *Scientific American* and Einstein's *Principle of Relativity* have reading levels around 12.

To estimate the reading level (L_r) of your writing, apply Equation A-1 to a paragraph of average length in the document:

$$L_r = 0.4\,(N_{ws} + P_{lw}), \qquad (A\text{-}1)$$

where N_{ws} is the number of words in the paragraph divided by the number of sentences, and P_{lw} is the percentage of long words (if 20 percent, then insert 20). Long words consist of all words having three syllables or more with the following exceptions: (1) proper names, (2) first words of sentences, (3) compound words such as *book-keeper*, and (4) verbs that acquire their third syllable from tense or number endings (*-ed* or *-es*). Do not become obsessed with this calculation. A good way to approach this calculation is as just a piece of evidence to help you decide whether the writing style is too complex.

redundancy (●) A redundancy is a needless repetition of a word or words within a sentence. Several redundancies are common in professional writing (note that the words in parentheses can be cut without loss of meaning):

(already) existing	empty (void)
(alternative) choices	first (began)
at (the) present (time)	introduced (a new)
(basic) fundamentals	mix (together)
(completely) eliminate	never (before)
(continue to) remain	none (at all)
(currently) underway	off (of)

reference citations (𝔍↔) Reference citations appear at the end of a document or section and take several forms. In a numbered system, they are listed in the order of appearance in the text. In an author–year system, they are listed alphabetically. As for the citation's form, there are several possibilities. A common form is to list the citation as a single sentence. Examples of this form are as follows:

Book	Author, *Title in Initial Capitals and Italics*, edition # (City of Publication: Publisher, Date of Publication), pp. #s.

Handbook of Chemistry and Physics, 50th ed. (New York: Chemical Rubber Company, 1969), p. 236.

Einstein, Albert, *Principle of Relativity* (New York: Dover, 1924), pp. 10, 14–21.

Halliday, David, and Robert Resnick, *Fundamentals of Physics*, revised printing (New York: Wiley, 1974).

Article   Author, "Title in Initial Capitals and Quotation Marks," *Journal Name in Italics*, vol. #, no. # (Date), pp. #s.

Houghton, R.A., and G.M. Woodwell, "Global Climatic Change," *Scientific American*, vol. 260, no. 4 (April 1989), p. 47.

Edwards, M., "Chernobyl—One Year After," *National Geographic*, vol. 171, no. 5 (1987), pp. 632–653.

Newspaper Author (if known), "Title in Initial Capitals and Quotation Marks," *Newspaper Name in Italics* (Date), sec. #, pp. #s.

"New Liner Titanic Hits an Iceberg; Sinking by the Bow at Midnight," *New York Times* (15 April 1912), p. 1.

Report   Author, *Title in Initial Capitals and Italics*, Report # (City of Publication: Publisher (Company or Agency), Date), pp. #s.

Report of the Presidential Commission on the Space Shuttle Challenger, vol. 1 (Washington, D.C.: US Government Printing Office, 1986).

Patent   Patent Holder, *Patent # in Italics* (Date of Patent).

Schawlow, Arthur L., and Charles H. Townes, *U.S. Patent No. 2,929,222* (22 March 1960).

Brochure Author, "Title in Initial Capitals and Quotation Marks," type of document (City of Publication: Publisher, Date), pp. #s.

League of Women Voters, "Nuclear Waste Primer," brochure (New York: Lyons & Burford, 1993).

Interview Speaker's Name, Speaker's Affiliation (City of Interview: Date of Interview), type of interview.

Ochoa, Ellen, NASA astronaut (Houston: 5 June 1997), telephone interview.

Letter   Author, Affiliation (City: Date of Letter), recipient of letter.

Alley, C.D., Plant Manager of Mason-Hanger Pantex Plant (Amarillo, TX: 3 March 1989), letter to *Amarillo Globe News*.

Web Site	Author, "Title," *web address in italics* (City: Sponsor, Date).

Gannon, Robert, "What Really Sank the Titanic," *http://www.popsci.com/context/features/titanic/* (Norwalk, CT: *Popular Science*, 1995).

Thole, Travis, "Exploring the Possibility of Primitive Life on Early Mars," *http://tc.engr.wisc.edu/uer/* (Madison, WI: University of Wisconsin, 1997).

"X-34 Model Makes First Captive Test Flight," *http://www.nasa.gov/* (Washington: NASA, 29 June 1999).

reference listings (𝕁↔) When incorporating the opinions, data, and illustrations of other sources into your writing, you must give credit to those sources. Several methods exist for bestowing that credit in the text: a numbered system, an author–year system, and an author–page number system. You should use a system that serves your document and is familiar to your audience. For instance, the sciences often use an author–year system because the author establishes where the information arose and the year identifies how current the information is. In such a system, this information is placed within brackets. Two possibilities are illustrated as follows:

> Recently, a new chemical process was developed for eliminating nitrogen oxide emissions from diesel engines [Perry and Siebers, 1986].

> Recently, Perry and Siebers [1986] developed a new chemical process for eliminating nitrogen oxide emissions from diesel engines.

For three or more authors, just list the first author's name as follows: [Lee and others, 1972]. If there is no author listed, give the first word (not articles, conjunctions, or prepositions) of the document: [*Manual*, 1983] or ["Plastic," 1989]. The full **reference citations** will appear in an alphabetical list at the end of your document.

Note that because a numbered system is less intrusive, you may select it when the audience does not require the names and dates of the sources at the moment of reading. The third system mentioned, the author–page number, is the one most often taught by English departments. Named the MLA (Modern Language Association) style (yet another confusing use of the word *style*), this system serves documents that discuss lengthy sources — say a comparison of characters in Hemingway's *A Farewell to Arms* and Andjaane's *The English Patient*. Unless you are making several references to a lengthy source, choose one of the first two systems.

run-on sentence (●) Sentences are the fundamental units of expression in scientific documents. Readers of professional writing expect authors to write in sentences. When a sentence runs on, readers often lose their place in the paragraph. They also lose confidence in the author.

The most common type of run-on sentence occurs when the writer tries to use an adverb such as *however, otherwise,* or *therefore* to join two independent clauses. In such cases, consider one of the following: (1) begin a second sentence; (2) join the clauses with a coordinating conjunction such as *and, or,* or *but;* or (3) make one of the clauses a dependent clause.

Mistake:	There is no cure for Alzheimer's, *however,* scientists have isolated the gene that causes it.
Correction:	There is no cure for Alzheimer's. However, scientists have isolated the gene that causes it.
Correction:	There is no cure for Alzheimer's, but scientists have isolated the gene that causes it.

Correction: Although there is no cure for Alzheimer's, scientists
have isolated the gene that causes it.

semicolon (●) The semicolon serves two purposes: to join two independent clauses closely linked in thought, and to separate items in a complex list. Given the inherent complexity of professional writing, many writers, including me, seldom use the semicolon for the first purpose. Most sentences in professional writing are taxing enough for the reader — why extend them? The semicolon, though, is valuable for separating items in a complicated list:

> The DOE is considering three sites for the nuclear waste repository: Yucca Mountain, Nevada; Deaf Smith County, Texas; and the Hanford Nuclear Reservation, Washington.

s/he (see **he or she**)

slash (✎)   To reduce needless complexity, you should avoid word constructions that incorporate slashes such as *he/she, s/he, w/o,* and *and/or*. For the first two examples, use plural pronouns (*they, them*) or **he or she**. In the case of *w/o*, simply write *without*. Finally, in the case of *and/or*, using either *or* or *and* suffices ninety-five percent of the time, and in those cases in which both are required, rely on plain English:

Detection calls for an MRI or a CAT scan or both.

split infinitive ( ) *To measure quickly* or *to quickly measure*, that is the question — whether it is an improvement to keep the infinitive together or to allow a single adverb to slide between. Language experts from the seventeenth century, striving to make English parallel with Latin, decided that it was important for infinitives to remain unbroken. Language experts today have decided that it is not. While keeping the infinitive together does slightly improve the sound of some sentences, this issue is not nearly as important as others. Besides, as Bernstein [1965] says, how would you correct a split infinitive such as "to almost double production"?

stratum, strata (see **medium, media**)

subject–verb disagreement (⬤) Each subject must agree in number with the verb. When you have a singular subject, readers expect you to use a singular verb, and when you have a plural subject, readers expect you to use a plural verb.

> Example: A series of shocks often precedes a large earthquake. *(Singular subject, singular verb.)*
>
> Example: Two aftershocks of the earthquake were almost as powerful as the earthquake itself. *(Plural subject, plural verb.)*

Deciding whether some subjects are singular or plural is not straightforward. For instance, compound subjects are sometimes treated as single units:

> Under these conditions, the simultaneous seeding of the fluid's flow and measuring of the fluid's temperature is difficult.

Also, some foreign words such as *criterion* (Greek), *phenomenon* (Greek), and *stratum* (Latin) have unusual plurals: *criteria, phenomena,* and *strata.*

> Mistake: The phenomena *was* studied.
>
> Correction: The phenomena were studied.

Moreover, words such as *none, some, number,* and *all* are singular in some instances, but plural in others.

Example: The number of observations was twenty.

Example: A number of observations were made.

Also tricky is determining the number of a verb following the phrase "one of." In the example below, you would use a singular verb to agree with the subject "one":

Example: In the sinking of the *Titanic*, one of the remaining mysteries is whether the *California* saw the distress flares of the sinking ship. *(singular verb "is")*

However, in a dependent clause that follows "one of the people who" or "one of the things that," choose a plural verb because the *who* refers to the plural noun *people* and the *that* refers to the plural noun *things*.

Example: The manned expedition to Mars is one of those projects that call on scientists and engineers to estimate how much advancement in technology will occur. *(plural verb "call")*

Finally, if the subject consists of two singular nouns joined by *or*, *either...or*, or *neither...nor*, the subject is singular and requires a singular verb.

Example: Neither oxygen nor nitrogen is a noble gas.

If the subject consists of two plural nouns joined by *or*, *either...or*, or *neither...nor*, the subject is plural and requires a plural verb.

Example: Neither ceramics nor gases conduct electricity at low voltages.

If the subject consists of a singular noun and a plural noun joined by *or*, *either...or*, or *neither...nor*, the number of the second noun determines whether the verb is singular or plural.

Example: Neither the pilot nor the crew members were present. *("Crew members" is plural; therefore, the verb is plural.)*

subjunctive mood (   ) A verb's subjunctive mood — as distinguished from the indicative mood, which states a fact,

and the imperative mood, which expresses a command —
is used in special circumstances, most often to state conditions that are improbable or contrary to fact.

> If the space ship *were* to attain a velocity near the speed of
> light, its mass would change.

Other examples of the subjunctive are in clauses following demands or desires:

> The manager demanded that the proposal *be* reviewed.
> I wish that I *were* going.
> If I *were* you, I would apply for the position.

symbols(✎) Some symbols, such as the dollar sign ($) and
percent symbol (%), are so common that audiences read
them without pausing. Other symbols, such as the slash
(/) and ampersand (&), cause audiences to pause. Still
others, such as the cent symbol (¢), lie in the gray. Because most symbols make the writing appear more complex, avoid them. Remember, though, that your degree
of avoidance depends on the symbol and the situation:

12 million dollars	equivalent to	$12 million
90 percent	equivalent to	90%
40 cents	preferable to	40¢
he or she	definitely better than	he/she, s/he
ebb and flow	definitely better than	ebb & flow

tables (🖅) Tables are row-and-column arrangements of
numbers or words. Unlike captions for **figures**, titles for
tables generally appear above the tables and in initial capitals (typically, they are single phrases). For an example,
see Table A-1. In the text, call tables by their names:
Table 1, Table 2, and so on. Another common table format has the title centered above the table.

Table A-1. Physical Characteristics of the Planets [*Handbook*, 1969]

Planet	Diameter (km)	Gravity (earth ratio)	Year (earth days)
Mercury	5,100	0.40	87.97
Venus	12,600	0.90	224.70
Earth	12,800	1.00	365.26
Mars	6,900	0.40	686.98
Jupiter	143,600	2.70	4,332.59
Saturn	120,600	1.20	10,759.20
Uranus	53,400	1.00	30,685.93
Neptune	49,700	1.00	60,187.64
Pluto	12,700	?	90,885

than, then (●) The word *than* is a conjunction that is used for comparisons: "The electrons move more quickly than the ions." The word *then* is an adverb that refers to time: "Then, we measured the current." Often confused, this word pair would be ranked as a major error except that most readers assume that any misuse is an error in typing, not knowledge.

that, which (●) In choosing between *that* and *which*, use *that* for defining clauses (often called necessary clauses because the information is needed to understand the sentence) and *which* for nondefining clauses (often called unnecessary clauses because the information is additional):

> We will select the option that has the highest thermal efficiency.
> *(the clause specifies which option)*
> We will select Option A, which has the highest thermal efficiency.
> *(the clause adds a fact about the known option)*

Notice that you separate nondefining *which* clauses from the rest of the sentence with commas. In addition to having nondefining *which* clauses follow nouns, many authors also have nondefining *which* clauses refer back to the idea of the sentence:

> The curve flattened, which shows that the projectile reached a peak velocity.

An interesting situation in which you might choose *which* rather than *that* is when you have two *that* clauses in the same sentence. In such instances, some writers use *which* for stylistic variation:

> They selected the option that had an operating value in a range which posed no danger.

typefaces (𝕱) A typeface (or font) is a shaped set of alphabetic letters. Hundreds of typefaces exist, a few of which appear in Table A-2. The typeface of a document says much about the document. For instance, the font Times conveys a sense of professionalism and authority (Times appears in several newspapers). Times belongs to a class of fonts known as serif fonts, which have projecting short strokes, such as the little feet on a serif "m." The other category of fonts is that of sans serif fonts, which do not have these projecting strokes (consider a sans serif "m"). One of the most common sans serif fonts is Helvetica.

In making choices of typefaces, you want to consider the subject matter, occasion, and audience. One font that is appropriate for the window display of a flower boutique may not be appropriate for the text of a report about flower germination. Given below are some general guidelines for choosing a typeface.

1. *Do not use too many typefaces in a document.* Some people mistakenly try to use all the typefaces on their comput-

Table A-2. Common Typefaces in Professional Documents

Typeface	Characters	Class	Uses
Antiqua	abcdefghijklmnop qrstuvwxyz	serif	text of formal documents
Old English	abcdefghijklmnop qrstubwxyz	serif	(out of date)
Palatino	abcdefghijklmnop qrstuvwxyz	serif	text of formal documents
Schoolbook	abcdefghijklmnop qrstuvwxyz	serif	text of formal documents
Times	abcdefghijklmnop qrstuvwxyz	serif	text of formal documents
Arial Narrow	abcdefghijklmnop qrstuvwxyz	sans serif	headings, text of informal documents
Helvetica	abcdefghijklmnop qrstuvwxyz	sans serif	headings, text of informal documents
Optima	abcdefghijklmnop qrstuvwxyz	sans serif	headings, text of informal documents

ers. What occurs in these situations is a mess. In a short document, such as a memo, one typeface suffices. In a longer document, you might use a serif font such as Times for the text and a sans serif font such as Arial Narrow for the headings and illustration call-outs. This combination works well—the sans serif font sets apart the headings and illustration call-outs from the text.

2. *Rely on serif fonts for the texts of formal documents.* If you look at most books and journals, you will see that publishers have used serif fonts for the text of the documents. For example, many newspapers use a variation of Times, and many textbooks use a variation of a font called Schoolbook. Note that newspapers, which have several columns,

often opt for Times because it is narrow. Textbooks are generally single-columned and are better suited for a wider font, such as Schoolbook.

Why not use sans serif fonts for the text of a document? One reason is that sans serif fonts do not have a connected baseline. This baseline makes it easier for the eye to jump from one line to the next, thereby preserving the continuity of the reading. For short lines, such as in a pamphlet, this jumping does not pose a problem. However, for longer lines, such as in a book, the reader benefits from the continuity that a serif font provides.

Another reason to use a serif font is tradition. Almost all professional books and journals have serif fonts as the typefaces of their texts. Moreover, because many publishers use sans serif fonts for the texts of grade-school readers, many people associate sans serif fonts with that class of writing. While some sans serif fonts such as Optima are acceptable for the texts of professional documents, many sans serif fonts such as Geneva are not.

3. *Be conservative with options such as boldface or italics.* Too much boldface will overwhelm a page and intimidate a reader. Italics, another typeface option, is also difficult to read in large blocks. Occasions in which boldface is appropriate are in headings and subheadings. With italics, appropriate uses include subheadings, glossary terms, foreign words, and accented sentences (such as commands in instructions). An underline is a poor person's substitute for italics. If your computer has italics, use it instead. Finally, shy away from cute options such as shadow or outline.

type sizes (𝕁) Type size is measured in points (a point is about 1/72 of an inch). Table A-3 gives occasions when various sizes of typefaces are used. As a general rule, use 12-point type for the text of documents that are single columned and use 10-point type for the text of documents that have multiple columns. For presentation visuals, use sizes between 18 and 36 points.

Table A-3. Uses for Different Sizes of Type

Size	Use
36 points	posters, visuals
24 points	posters, visuals
18 points	posters, visuals, titles
14 points	titles, headings
12 points	text, illustration call-outs
10 points	text, illustration call-outs
< 10 points	footnotes

typo (●) A typographical error is an error such as a missing or incorrectly spelled word that spell-checker could not catch (*tall* as opposed to *talk*). Although audiences are generally more forgiving about these errors than they are about errors that a spell-checker could catch, you should work to avoid them, particularly in high-profile portions of documents, such as titles, and in places such as numerals in which the typo changes the meaning.

unclear pronoun reference (●) Many ambiguities arise because of mistakes with pronouns. According to Fowler's *A Dictionary of Modern English Usage* [1965], an important principle for using pronouns is that there should not be "even a momentary doubt" as to what the pronoun refers to. Many scientists and engineers, unfortunately, ignore this principle. They abuse pronouns, particularly the pronouns *it* and *this*. For more discussion, refer back to my pet peeve for the naked *this* in Chapter 3.

unique, when preceded by very (●) The word *unique* is an absolute that does not need a modifier. Either something is unique or it is not. For that reason, the phrase "very unique" makes no sense. Another absolute is the word *critical*. Therefore, shun phrases such as "most critical."

verb tense (●) In a document, you should maintain the same reference frame for the tenses of verbs. In other words, if in a document, you assume that an event occurred in the past, then that event should remain in the past for the entire document:

> **Experiment.** The experiment consisted of a Wolfhard–Parker burner in a stainless-steel container. The burner slot for the fuel flow was rectangular and was surrounded on all sides by passages for flow of air. Previous experiments had shown that such a geometry provides a nearly two-dimensional flame.

Because the first sentence places the experiment in the past tense, all details in this section occurring during the experiment are in the past tense, and all details occurring before the time of the experiment are in the pluperfect tense (for example, "had shown"). Notice that the last detail ("provides") is in the present tense because it is a time-independent fact.

Should the writer choose to have the experiment occur in the present tense, the reference frame shifts up one notch, as do all verbs except those presenting time-independent facts.

> **Experiment.** The experiment consists of a Wolfhard–Parker burner in a stainless-steel container. The burner slot for the fuel flow is rectangular and is surrounded on all sides by passages for flow of air. Previous experiments have shown that such a geometry provides a nearly two-dimensional flame.

we (see **first person**)

which (see **that, which**)

who, whom (⬤) In the old days, you used *who* for the nominative case (usually the subject of a clause), and *whom* for all other cases (usually the direct object of the clause or the object of a preposition within the clause). Examples are as follows with the clauses in italics:

> Kris has to decide *who will receive the promotion.* (subject of clause)
> Angie was the one *whom Kris chose.* (direct object—"Kris" is the subject of the clause)
> Don't ask *for whom the bell tolls.* (object of preposition—"bell" is the subject of the clause)

So far, so good. However, some sentences are tricky:

> *Whom will you choose?* (direct object—"you" is the subject of the clause)
> Angie was the one *who* Kris decided *should receive the promotion.* (subject of clause—"should receive" is the verb of the clause, and "Kris decided" is a separate clause)
> I will award this proposal to *whoever has the lowest bid.* (subject of

clause — note that preposition "to" is not part of the dependent clause)

In everyday conversation, many choose *who* over *whom* no matter what the situation. Because so many people speak this way, even when *whom* is the correct choice, it has begun to sound unusual, even erudite, especially when it is the first word in the sentence. In fact, one person running for a senate seat in Wisconsin changed a campaign ad from the correct usage ("Whom will you support?") to the incorrect usage ("Who will you support?") because the correct usage sounded "uppity."

In his column "On Language" in the *New York Times*, William Safire [1997] advises that you should use *whom* for the direct object, indirect object, and object of prepositions in a clause, unless *whom* is the first word of the sentence. In that case, use *who*. Note, though, that more conservative publications such as the *Wall Street Journal* still begin sentences with *whom*.

In a sense, our language is evolving much as a species evolves. This evolution of language is not based on survival of the fittest, but survival of the most efficient. Having just the simple word *who* is more efficient than having to choose between the two words *who* and *whom*. Perhaps if *whom* served a purpose in determining the meaning of a sentence, it would survive, but its role in the evolution of language is similar to the role of the appendix in the evolution of the human body — providing little utility, only pain. For that reason, this word's days are numbered. If not for a beautiful line in a poem, this word might already be gone.

Bibliography

Bernstein, Theodore M., *The Careful Writer: A Modern Guide to English Usage* (New York: Atheneum, 1965).

Cook, Claire Kehrwald, *Line by Line: How to Edit Your Own Writing* (Boston: Modern Language Association of America, 1985).

Eisenberg, Anne, *Guide to Technical Editing* (New York: Oxford, 1992).

Fowler, H.W., *A Dictionary of Modern English Usage*, 2nd ed. (Oxford: Oxford University Press, 1983).

Funk, Robert, Elizabeth McMahan, and Susan Day, *The Elements of Grammar for Writers* (New York: Macmillan, 1991).

Graves, Robert, and Alan Hodge, *The Use and Abuse of the English Language* (New York: Marlowe and Company, 1970).

Hacker, Diane, *Rules for Writers*, 3rd edition (Boston: Bedford Books, 1996).

The Chicago Manual of Style, 14th ed. (Chicago: The University of Chicago Press, 1993).

O'Connor, Patricia T., *Woe Is I* (New York: Grosset/Putnam, 1996).

Sabin, William A., *The Gregg Reference Manual*, 8th edition (New York: McGraw-Hill, 1996).

Safire, William, "On Language," *The New York Times Magazine* (6 April 1997), p. 18.

Sandia National Laboratories, *Format Guidelines for Sandia Reports*, SAND90-9001 (Livermore, California: Sandia National Laboratories, 1990).

Skillin, Marjorie E., and Robert M. Gay, *Words Into Type*, 3rd edition (New York: Prentice-Hall, 1974).

Strunk, Jr., William, and E.B. White, *Elements of Style*, 3rd edition (New York: Macmillan, 1979).

Wilson, Kenneth G., *The Columbia Guide to Standard American English* (New York: Columbia University Press, 1993).

Glossary of Editing Terms

Like many subjects, editing contains a wealth of specific terms: *recto, em-spaces, noun,* and *verb.* Are these terms really valuable to know? I believe that they are. While formatting terms such as *recto* and *em-spaces* are not necessary for you to know in dealing with authors, they are handy to know in your dealings with communication professionals: artists, compositors, and technical writers. As for grammatical terms such as *noun* and *verb,* knowing them strengthens your hand in explaining and defending many editorial decisions. For instance, how can you explain when to use *affect* and *effect* if you do not know what a noun and verb are? Or how can you explain when to use *who* and *whom* if you do not know what a subject and object are?

Many grammatical terms belong to a core of knowledge that, as E.D. Hirsch [1996] asserts, all English-speaking people should possess to function effectively in our society. For you as an editor, possessing this core of knowledge does not mean that you must have a textbook definition of each term. Rather, possessing this core means that you can understand and correctly use these terms in your dealings with others.

active voice: a verb form in which the subject performs the action in the sentence: "Jackals *attacked* a wildebeest calf."

adjective: a word that modifies a noun or pronoun: "Scientists were surprised when the *huge* earthquake and *unexpected* landslide triggered such a *massive* eruption."

adverb: a word that modifies a verb, adjective, or another adverb: "When Mount Pelée erupted, the lava gushed *so rapidly* through Saint-Pierre that *only* two citizens survived."

appositive: a noun or noun phrase placed next to a noun to define or explain that noun: "*A condition resembling intoxication,* nitrogen narcosis affects divers at depths of 30 meters or more."

back matter: the sections of a report (or book) following the text. Examples are the appendices and the glossary. Other parts of a report are the **front matter** and **main text**.

bleed: to extend to the end of the page, often occurring with an illustration or an air-brush.

bullet: the symbol • placed before each term in a list.

call-out: a label that identifies part of an illustration

camera-ready copy: document that is ready for offset printing.

clause: a group of words containing a subject and a finite verb. A clause may be dependent, meaning that it cannot stand alone as a sentence ("when elephants search for food") or independent, meaning that it can stand alone as a sentence ("elephants communicate to one another by making rumbling noises similar to gargling").

condensed type: type that is thin in proportion to its height — example of condensed type.

conjunction: a word that joins words, phrases, or clauses. There are three types of conjunctions: coordinating, correlative, and subordinating. Coordinating conjunctions (*and, but, or, nor*) join words, phrases, and clauses of equal rank. Generally, these are the words that people mean when they say the word "conjunction." Correlative conjunctions are simply coordinating conjunctions used in pairs (*both...and, not only...but (also), either...or, neither...nor*) to join words, phrases, and clauses of equal rank. Subordinating conjunctions are words such as *because, although*, and *when* that introduce dependent (or subordinating) clauses.

connotation: the implied or associated meaning of a word.

content: the message that the author intends to communicate.

continuous tone: picture, such as a photograph, made of modulated shades of gray or color.

crop: to cut away parts of an illustration, often a photograph, to fit into a desired space or to remove unwanted detail.

denotation: the dictionary meaning of a word.

dependent clause: a clause that cannot stand alone as a sentence. These clauses begin with subordinating conjunctions such as "although," "when," "because," and "if": "*Because anemometers are so delicate,* they cannot be used to measure directly the wind speeds of tornadoes."

direct object (see **object**)

doublet: a word occurring twice in succession where only one occurrence was intended ("The vaccine combated *the the* virus").

em-space: the amount of space taken up by the letter m (the length of an em-dash would be the length of the letter m).

en-space: the amount of space taken up by the letter n (the length of an en-dash would be the length of the letter n).

finite verb (see **verb**)

folio: page number.

form: the format, grammar, punctuation, spelling, and usage of the writing.

format: the way in which a document is arranged. Format includes such things as the choice of typeface, the spacing between sections, and the referencing system for sources. In professional writing, there is no single ordained format. Whatever company you work for or whatever journal you submit to, you should arrange your document or presentation to meet that company's or journal's format.

front matter: the sections of a report (or book) preceding the main text. Examples of sections in the front matter are the title page, the foreword, the acknowledgments, and the table of contents.

gerund: a present participle that functions as a noun: "Walking is great exercise." Often, the gerund is part of a phrase that serves as a noun: "In scuba diving, *ascending too quickly* will not allow your body enough time to dispose of the nitrogen that it has absorbed."

grammar: the rules of writing that dictate how words are to be arranged into sentences. Actually, English, when compared with other languages such as German, does not have many rules of grammar. English does, though, have a host of rules for usage.

gutter: the inside margin of facing pages; the binding edge of the page.

halftone: any picture reproduced from continuous-tone originals by a pattern of dots or lines of various sizes and degrees of proximity.

illustration: the meshing of words and images in a document. Illustration includes not only the presence of figures and tables, but also the captions of those figures and tables as well as the introductions of those figures and tables in the text.

imperative mood: a command form of a verb in which the subject is an understood "you." An example is *"Turn* on the computer." The subject of this sentence is "you," even though the word "you" is not explicitly in the sentence.

indirect object: a noun or pronoun that names to whom or for whom the action of the clause is done: "NSF awarded *our lab* the contract."

infinitive phrase: a verb phrase in which the verb is coupled with the word "to": *"To calculate the energy,* you multiply the frequency by Planck's constant."

introductory series: a list of nouns at the beginning of a sentence that defines the subject of the sentence. The introductory series is separated from the rest of the sentence by a dash: *"Nitrogen narcosis, decompression sickness, and arterial gas embolism –* these are the greatest dangers facing scuba divers."

jargon: a word, abbreviation, or slang term that is particular to a company, laboratory, or group. Within the company, laboratory, or group, the expressions can be an efficient shorthand for communicating information. However, to outside readers, the expressions are often alienating.

justification: alignment of the lines relative to the margins. Left justification means that the text lines up straight on the left margin; right justification means that the text lines up straight on the right margin. Fully justified text means that the text aligns itself straight on both margins.

kerning: the degree of overlap among characters of the same line.

language: the way we use words in writing and speaking. Language is more than just vocabulary; it includes the order of words, the lengths of sentences, and the use of examples.

leading: the amount of space between lines.

main text: the sections of a report from the "Introduction" through the "Conclusions." In general, the main text should stand alone as a document written to the primary audience of the report.

mechanics: grammar, punctuation, spelling, and usage.

noun: a word that identifies an action, person, place, quality, or thing. Examples include "flight," "scientist," "laboratory," "curiosity," and "oscilloscope."

object: a noun, pronoun, or noun phrase that receives the action of the verb ("The viper bit *my leg*").

participle: a special form of a verb. Present participles end in "-ing" (*working*) and past participles often end in "-ed" (*worked*). Participles and participial phrases often serve as modifiers: "*Hunting at night*, the *tagged* tiger was rarely seen *making a kill*." When a present participle serves as a noun ("*Swimming* burns many calories"), it is called a **gerund**.

passive voice: a verb form in which the subject does not act, but is acted upon: "The wildebeest calf *was attacked* by jackals." Note that the emphasis of the paper from which this example arises is on wildebeests, not jackals.

phrase: a group of words that may contain a subject or finite verb, but not both. Examples include prepositional phrases ("of open grasslands"), participial phrases ("foraging for food"), and infinitive phrases ("to warn others in the herd").

pica: a unit of measurement equal to 12 points, or roughly 1/6 of an inch.

point: a unit of measure for the size of type (1 point $\approx$ 1/72 of an inch). The text of most documents is set in type sizes between 10 and 12 points.

predicate nominative: a noun, pronoun, or noun phrase that follows the verb "to be" and renames or identifies the subject: "The star was actually *a cluster of stars*."

preposition: a part of speech that indicates a relationship such as time, manner, or place between its object and another word in the sentence. Examples include *about, above across, after, against, beside, between, beyond, by, despite, down, in, inside, like, near, of, through, to, until, upon* and *with.* Prepositions introduce noun phrases that bring these details of time, manner, and place into sentences: "*within* a few hours," "*with* much speed," and "*under* the bridge."

pronoun: a part of speech that may be used instead of a noun. Examples are "I," "he," "she," "it," "we," and "they."

punctuation: the rules of writing governing the use of the period, question mark, exclamation point, colon, semicolon, comma, dash, apostrophe, ellipsis marks, slash, and quotation marks.

recto: odd-numbered pages in a document.

river: distracting spacing within paragraphs (usually between words) that sometimes occurs when type is set fully justified.

roman: normal typeface (not italics or boldface).

sans serif: a type style, such as Helvetica or Arial Narrow, in which no short strokes stem from the upper and lower ends of letters. Sans serif fonts are often used in posters, visuals, and illustrations.

scope: the boundaries of a document or presentation. Scope includes what the document or presentation will cover.

sentence: a group of words with a subject and verb (finite) that expresses a complete thought. Sentences often contain an object that receives the action of the verb: "The virus attacked the cell." Here, *virus* is the subject, *attacked* is the verb, and *cell* is the object. To this sentence you can add adjectives, adverbs, phrases, and dependent clauses. While a subject and verb appear in every sentence, an object does not.

series comma: the comma that appears before the conjunction preceding the last term in a series of three or more items. As an example, consider the series "oxygen, hydrogen, and carbon." The series comma in this example is the comma after *hydrogen.* Some types of writing such as journalism avoid the series comma. (See discussion of "commas in a series" in the Appendix.)

serif: a type style, such as Times or Schoolbook, in which short strokes stem from the upper and lower ends of letters. This book has been typeset in a serif font called Book Antiqua.

split infinitive: the placement of a word or words between the word *to* and the verb of an infinitive phrase — for example, "to slowly raise" as opposed to "to raise slowly." (See the discussion in the Appendix.)

structure: the strategy of your writing. Structure includes the organization of details, the transition between details, the depth of details, and the emphasis of details.

style: (1) the way that you present information in your writing (including such aspects as the way you organize details, the words you select, and the illustrations you choose); (2) a modifier appearing before the word "manual" or "guide" that refers to those aspects of writing — particularly language, format, punctuation, and usage — that are not universal in form.

subject: who or what the sentence or clause is about. The subject usually consists of a noun or pronoun and its complements ("*Some fuel* is usually left unburned in the tank"). However, a subject can also be a phrase ("Unfortunately, *estimating the exact amount of fuel left in the tank* is impossible") or even a clause ("*What fuel was left in the tank* must have caused the explosion").

syntax: the ordering of words within a sentence.

tone: whatever in the writing indicates the attitude of the writer toward the subject.

usage: the rules of writing governing the proper use of words — for example, whether to use *affect* or *effect* in a sentence.

verb: a word that indicates an action or a state of being within a sentence: "The shock *shattered* the volcano's summit and *was* responsible for the collapse of the mountain's north side." Finite verbs are capable of making assertions ("fuel *burns*"), while nonfinite verbs (such as **participles** and **infinitives**) are not ("fuel *burning*" or "fuel *to burn*").

verso: even-numbered pages in a document.

widow: a single line, from the end of a paragraph, appearing at the top of a printed page or column. Widows are to be avoided in the layout of a document.

References

Alley, Michael, *The Craft of Scientific Writing*, 3rd edition (New York: Springer-Verlag, 1996).

American Society of Mechanical Engineers (ASME), "Suggestions to the Reviewer," version 98/99 (New York: International Gas Turbine Institute, 1998).

Angell, Marcia, *Science on Trial: the Clash of Medical Evidence and the Law in the Breast Implant Case* (New York: Norton, 1996), pp. 58–59.

Brander, Roy, "The Titanic Disaster: An Enduring Example of Money Management Versus Risk Management," *http://www.cuug.ab.ca:8001/~branderr/risk_essay/titanic.html* (Calgary: Calgary Unix Users Group, 1995).

Bullard, Fred M., "Types of Volcanic Eruptions," *Volcanoes of the Earth*, rev. ed. (Austin: University of Texas Press, 1976), p. 266.

"The Case of the $70 Million Comma," *The Financial Times* (19 June 1999).

The Chicago Manual of Style, 14th edition (Chicago: University of Chicago Press, 1993).

Cook, Claire Kehrwald, *Line by Line: How to Edit Your Own Writing* (Boston: Modern Language Association of America, 1985).

Forbes, Malcolm, "How to Write a Business Letter" (Elmsford, NY: International Paper Company, 1979).

Fowler, H.W., *A Dictionary of Modern English Usage*, 2nd ed. (Oxford: Oxford University Press, 1965), pp. 481, 579.

Gannon, R., "What Really Sank the Titanic," *Popular Science*, vol. 246 (February 1995), pp. 49–55, 83.

Gunning, R., *The Technique of Clear Writing* (New York: McGraw-Hill, 1952).

Handbook of Chemistry and Physics, 50th ed. (New York: Chemical Rubber Company, 1969), p. 236.

Hirsch, E.D., *The Schools We Need and Why We Don't Have Them* (New York: Doubleday, 1996).

Maugham, Somerset, *Of Human Bondage* (1915).

"Die neue Rechtschreibung," *Die Woche*, extra section (May 1997).

Rhodes, Richard, *How to Write* (New York: Quill, 1995), p. 113.

Safire, William, "On Language," *The New York Times Magazine* (6 April 1997), p. 17.

Sandia National Laboratories, *Format Guidelines for Sandia Reports*, SAND90-9001 (Livermore, California: Sandia National Laboratories, 1990).

Seneca, *Epistulae ad Lucilium*.

Stevenson, Robert Louis, quotation attributed.

Strunk, Jr., William, and E.B. White, *Elements of Style*, 3rd edition (New York: Macmillan, 1979).

Van Buren, Robert, and Mary Fran Buehler, "The Levels of Edit," 2nd edition, *Jet Propulsion Laboratory Publication 80-1* (Los Angeles: California Institute of Technology, 1980).

Index